D1283895

Live the Life You Have Always Dreamed Of!

by
Chris Widener

What others are saying about Chris Widener...

"I have spoken to more than 3,000 audiences and I can tell you that Chris Widener is one of the best speakers in America today. He has wonderful content -- extremely motivational, he is funny, he is sharp, he is quick and to the point. You'll love him too."
-- Brian Tracy, author of Eat That Frog

"Our people loved Chris and loved his material. He was extremely helpful and challenging. My sales team and I highly recommend him!"
-- Phil Castillo, Director, Northern Channels,
Cisco Systems

"Chris Widener has the talent, the articulation, the message, the presence, the ability! Chris Widener is one of the brand new top stars on the International platform speaking circuit today."
-- Denis Waitley, author of Seeds of Greatness

I was surprised at how quickly I was able to apply the practical principles in both my personal and professional life. Chris has done an excellent job of organizing his material and packaging it in a thought-provoking, compelling, professional, and timely presentation. I consider his seminar extremely worthwhile and I wholeheartedly recommend it to anyone.
-- Michael Lienau President,
Global Net Productions, Video and Film

"Chris Widener is nothing short of phenomenal. His patience, his knowledge, his ability to engage with an audience; Chris, you do an amazing job."
-- Jim Rohn, author of The Five Major Pieces to the Life Puzzle

Chris' material is strategic, yet simple to apply. It will change you and the organization you work with. It made a difference for us!
-- Jamie Bland, VP Strategic Alliances, Innuity

"Chris Widener is a powerful presenter, a quick wit, and a home run every time. He definitely challenges you to the next level in life and work."
-- Kevin Mather, CFO, Seattle Mariners Baseball Team

I read both of your books, The Angel Inside and Twelve Pillars – I couldn't put them down. All I can say is WOW! Both books spoke to me in many ways. It is guaranteed that I am going to be re-reading them again and again, as I am sure more lessons will come to me each time. I am going to be printing off the 10 "Principles" from "The Angel Inside" as well as the "12 Pillars of Success" and putting them on my desk so I see them every day. Thanks again.
-- Pam Steciuk

The sooner you can take in these incredible success principles that Chris teaches through his books and seminars, and apply them in your life, the sooner you can share them with others, which is where the true gift lies.
-- Donna Johnson, Executive National Vice President, Arbonne International

Published by
Chris Widener International and YourSuccessStore.com
www.ChrisWidener.com
www.YourSuccessStore.com

Distributed by
www.YourSuccessStore.com
2835 Exchange Boulevard
Suite 200
Southlake, Texas 76092
877-929-0439

Live the Life You Have Always Dreamed Of! / Chris Widener

ISBN: 0-9726266-0-3   Paperback
ISBN: 0-9726266-5-4   Hardback

Printed in The United States of America

Live the Life You Have Always Dreamed Of!
Contents

Dedication

Dedicated to all of those who have a dream of a better life, that they may have the courage and persistence to pursue that dream until it becomes a reality!

Foreword
It's True Because I've Lived It

I haven't always been what I am now. I haven't always done what I do now. I haven't always had what I have now. No, this story starts a long time ago and a great distance from the life I live now.

Imagine if this were your life:

Imagine being born to a couple where the man doesn't even want you. In fact, he pressured your mother into having an abortion, which she refused. Talk about mixed blessings! On one hand you get to live, but on the other you have a father who doesn't even want you. Not the preferred way to be brought into the world, is it?

Then imagine four years later when that father dies after a short battle with cancer. You are just four years old, and left without a father. As a young boy, you are rudderless, left to find your way to manhood alone. What is worse, what deepens the impact of the death is that the father who never wanted you goes to his grave without leaving so much as a note saying, "I'll miss you." Or "I'm sorry I won't be able to see you grow up."

You grow up bitter and angry. Soon you begin to act out in destructive ways. Your mother does the best she can to raise you but she is gone much of the time, working to provide for you. You are comfortably lower middle class.

When you are in just sixth grade you fall into the wrong crowd. You begin to break the law, take drugs and drink alcohol. Just 12 years old and already headed down the wrong path. In seventh grade you smoke marijuana regularly. This explains your nearly failing grade point average. Your principal passes you on to the eighth grade, not because you deserve it, but to get rid of you sooner.

Fortunately, you play sports, and you play them well. They are most likely what keeps you from going so far over the edge as to not return. Sports provide another positive impact: Your job during your teenage years is working with a professional basketball team. It is the highlight of every day.

Junior high and high school are a pain because you are a pain to the teachers and they in turn discipline you. It seems as though it is one big war. You wonder where your life is going. The lack of control and direction only serves to make you angrier and more and more bitter.

When you are sixteen you pick up a book about a career you are interested in. You read it and are amazed. You love the idea. You wonder if it is possible. You dream. Your dream is to one day become a professional speaker-- to stand before the masses and inspire, motivate, and challenge them. You want to make something of yourself so you can tell others that no matter how difficult it may be, they can make something of themselves as well.

When you are seventeen you have a monumental experience in your life where everything changes one hundred and eighty degrees. Your grades shoot up your senior year. You are able to go to college to study what you want and pursue the career you desire.

All along the way there are naysayers. There are people who do not believe you can do what you want. There are those who, while awake, are truly comatose to life. They do not actually live. They are dead but simply waiting for life to stop. They do not dream.

What would you think of this life? How would you live it? I ask, because this is my life. Yes, now I live in my beautiful dream home, I have a wonderful wife and four truly delightful and healthy children. I am surrounded by friends and colleagues who are some of the finest and most talented people there are on this old planet of ours. I make great money doing what I love to do. I speak to crowds all around America. I host a nationally televised show and co-host another with a legend in our industry: Zig Ziglar. My books sell like hotcakes. It's a great life.

But it wasn't always so.

No, I *chose* this life. I made decisions all along the way that brought me here. I lived out the principles you are about to read. You see, there are many "posers" out there who would teach you "success" principles but who have never lived them out themselves. It is one thing to regurgitate someone else's writings – it is another to learn for yourself the principles of successfully achieving all that you want to achieve and then to share them with others.

I know the principles you are about to read work because I have lived them. They are not pie in the sky, motivational, human potential fluff! They are practical steps to reaching the dream you have for your life.

Now, before you is a choice: You can continue to live among the walking dead, or you can come to life, no matter how old you may be, and run toward your dream. I am living mine, and I want to help you live yours.

Let's go!

Introduction

Take a moment right now to do something. Close your eyes and dream for a moment. Shut your eyes and imagine life as it could be. Imagine life as it would look if you had the life you really, truly desire. Do you see it? Can you see the people? Can you hear the sounds? Can you *feel* it? Is there a rich vividness to it? Wouldn't life be grand if we could only live it in reality as we see it in our minds when we dream? Yet, more often then not, we let ourselves dream, and then we open our eyes, shake our heads, and tell ourselves, "Now I need to get back to reality."

For some people, the life we dream of *is* a reality! Why? Because they are better than us? Because they deserve it more than we do? Because they are luckier than we are? Absolutely not! There is a reason though, why some people are living *our* dreams. Because they did what it takes to make their dreams a reality. They went beyond just wishing and they began to *create*! They created the life they wanted. They took action control to live the life they wanted. They took responsibility for their own destiny. And now you can too!

I am a firm believer in the theory that, with just a very few exceptions, we all live exactly the lives we choose. This means that we can choose to have a different life the same way we have chosen to have the life we currently live. It makes sense, doesn't it? We all made conscious decisions to do certain things that got us right where we are today. Most of us went to college and chose a major, and then chose a career, then chose a company. We chose!

Now, if you don't like your life, make a choice to change it!

13

"But Chris, you just don't understand! I can't just quit my job!"

Let's start there. Yes, you can. The first mistake most people make is in the language they use that betrays a mindset that will keep them right where they are – in a place they don't want to be. Here is the key:

Don't mistake "I can't" when you mean, "I won't."

Let's take another look: "I won't just quit my job because I am scared I will starve."

"I won't just quit my job because I don't want to go back to college and spend two years of my life preparing for a new career."

"I won't just quit my job because I don't want to try my new career while I deliver pizzas at night to support myself."

"I won't just quit my job because I am afraid I'll look like a stupid failure."

You get the point. The idea is that we CAN do anything we choose to. We really mean that we can't because we won't. Once we get beyond this, we can really move toward our dream and live the life we always wanted to!

With that in mind, let's take a look at a few steps for pursuing your dream and living your new life:

Reconnect with your dream. Set aside some time to let yourself dream. What have you placed on the backburner in order to live the status quo? Settle on one or two dreams that you can and will pursue. Don't come up with too many. That will only deter you further.

Decide that you will do it. This may seem elementary, but many people never decide and commit fully to their dream. They simply keep "thinking" about it.

Tell others that you are going to do it. This puts you on the record as to what you are dreaming about. It makes you accountable. It will help you do it if for no other reason than to avoid embarrassment!

Develop a step-by-step plan. This is absolutely essential. You must sit down and write out a few things:

A timeline. How long will it take to the end?

Action steps. Point-by-point what you will do and when you will do them.

Resources you will need to draw from. What will it take? Who will need to be involved for help or advice?

An evaluation tool. You need to evaluate from time to time whether you are progressing or not.

A celebration. Yep, when you are done you should already have planned what you will do to celebrate. Make it big!

You CAN live any life that you choose. You CAN have the life you have always wanted. But you must decide that you will have it and then get on with pursuing it! There is still time. Go for it!

Preface
Take Ownership of Your Life

There are lots of things we desire to own in this life, aren't there? Many of them are fine and dandy, as the saying goes. But there is the most important thing we own that many people never think about owning, and that is their life! They spend a lot of time thinking about the next set of golf clubs, a vacation home, or a new piece of jewelry, but they never really understand that they own their life. Whenever it comes time to be responsible, they end up placing the blame somewhere else, rather than realizing that they are the owner and so they are responsible! With that in mind, here are some thoughts about the ownership your have of your life:

You only own one person – you. You don't own your spouse. You don't own your boss. You don't own your kids (with kids, you are in charge of them, given the tremendous responsibility of teaching them to own their own lives, but you don't own them). No, there is only one person you own, and that is you. That is great news! Now you don't have to worry about running anybody else's life! This is a temptation for us isn't it? We just know how everybody else should do it, and with many of them we try to take ownership and run their life! Well, hands off! Take control of your own life since it is the only one you own. You wouldn't try to drive somebody else's car from the grocery store parking lot, so don't try to drive their life either! You own you – so stick to you!

You get to choose what to do with only one person – you. Once you have come to realize that you only own you, you get to get to the fun part – running your life and making it what you want it to be. Instead of choosing what other people should do, you get to focus on choosing what you get to do. You get to begin to shape and mold your life. This is exciting! Aren't you glad you don't have to run everybody else's lives anymore? I am!

Your ownership means that you can do what you want with yourself. Your life is a blank sheet of paper. You can choose whatever you want to do. You can have whatever profession you want. You can earn as much money as you desire. You can marry whoever suits your fancy (as long as you suit their fancy too, by the way). Stop wishing and start choosing. I like to use the example of a person who is thirty years old and doesn't like their income. I tell them that if they so chose, they could go back to school, get a degree, go to medical school and by age forty be in a high-income profession. Then they would have 25 years of high wages to support the lifestyle they desire. You can choose whatever you want and take whatever actions you choose to rectify any situation you are in!

Your ultimate destination in life is set by you, not somebody else. Where will you end up? Wherever you choose to end up. You will do well to get it in your mind that some day you will be seventy years old and you will be at a certain place, and the only thing that got you there was the choices you made all along the way. Imagine that. If

> *Most people overestimate what they can do in a year, but underestimate what they can do in ten years.*
>
> *Anthony Robbins*

you are thirty, you have forty years – FORTY YEARS – of choices that can put you right where you want to be at the end of your life! So you're fifty-five? Who cares? You probably have at least twenty years left! You still have TWENTY YEARS to get yourself to whatever destination you choose. Do you know what a person can do in twenty years? ALMOST ANYTHING THEY SET THEIR HEART ON!

The responsibility for your life, and what you accomplish, is found in one person – you. You will accomplish what you choose to accomplish. You will make and save as much money as you choose to. You will write as many books as you choose to. You will take as many vacations as you choose to. You will have the kind of relationships you choose to. What you accomplish is up to you! Take that seriously!

Focus on your values and live them out, regardless of what other people do. This is key. We do not live our lives in a vacuum. We need to be very thoughtful about what we believe, about what our values are, and what our morality is. These things will all shape how we go about exerting ownership of our lives. But once we have come to understand these things for ourselves, the power to live our lives increases tremendously. Now it doesn't matter what anybody else does. It doesn't matter what the circumstances are. We live out of our morality, values and beliefs. These are the principles that transcend everything else and enable us to set our course!

I know this seems like a lot of responsibility, but I consider it a freedom and a privilege! We get one life to live and we get to shape it however we want. That is one job I want to take seriously and not mess up! With diligence, hard work, and a lot of right decisions, I'll get to the end of my life deeply fulfilled. I hope you will to!

Live the Life Principles

Principle Number One: DARE TO DREAM – When you choose to let your heart dream, and you pursue that dream, you are taking the first step in taking that dream from being something that exists in your mind and heart and making it into the life that you lead, live, and enjoy, each day.

Principle Number Two: VISION IS THE CORNERSTONE – Vision is the spectacular that motivates us to live out the mundane each day as we pursue our dreams. Vision gives us the big picture that causes us to live the little picture until the big picture becomes our reality.

Principle Number Three: GOALS ARE FOR ACHIEVING – Goals are the powerful carrot that leads the horse onward. Goals become a powerful force for action and change, luring and enticing us forward until we live our dreams.

Principle Number Four: THE TENACIOUS BIRD GETS THE WORM – It isn't the early bird. It isn't the strongest or smartest bird. It isn't the fastest bird. The bird that usually gets the worm is the one that sticks it out. Tenaciousness is a must for those who would achieve their dreams.

Principle Number Five: STAY MOTIVATED FOR SUCCESS – Those who can keep themselves motivated are the people who will enable themselves to live their dreams because they will keep themselves in a state that drives them toward their desired life.

Principle Number Six: IT REALLY IS BETTER TO GIVE THAN TO RECEIVE – Those who desire true success, not just financial success, are people who realize the positive force of good that is unleashed when they become people who give of their time, money, energy, and resources to make the world around them a better place.

Principle Number Seven: RELATIONSHIPS ARE THE CORE OF OUR EXISTENCE – Life is not lived alone. Every day of our lives depends on our ability to get along with, work with, and enjoy the people around us, whether it is our family, our friends, or our colleagues. Those who harness the power of relationships understand and enjoy the fruit of the core of human existence.

Principle Number Eight: DON'T TIP – KEEPING YOUR BALANCE – While pursuing your dreams it is easy to tip out of balance, to let an important area of life get out of whack. People who end their lives well, those who live their dreams, are people who maintain a healthy balance in their lives, keeping a positive tension between body, soul and spirit.

Principle Number Nine: ACHIEVE FINANCIAL FREEDOM – Financial freedom has nothing to do with how much money you have. While there are some basic understandings of how money works in terms of making and saving it, the key to living your dreams and enjoying life is to understand the truth of financial freedom. It lies in the difference between you having money, and money having you.

Principle Number Ten: ATTITUDE IS KING – Whatever your attitude is about life, it will directly affect the kind of life you have and what you achieve. In fact, your attitude will rule and reign over it. Your attitude is king and determines whether or not you will live the life you dream of.

Live the Life
Principle Number One:
DARE TO DREAM

Dare to Dream Again

"Far better it is to dare mighty things, to win glorious triumphs, even though checkered by failure, than to take rank with those poor spirits who neither enjoy nor suffer much, because they live in the gray twilight that knows neither victory nor defeat."
Teddy Roosevelt

Do you remember when you were a child and no dream seemed too big? Some of us thought we would walk on the moon; some dreamed of riding with Roy Rogers; others imagined stepping to the plate in a big-league game. Every one of us, when we were young, had a common trait - we were dreamers. The world hadn't gotten to us yet to show us that we couldn't possibly achieve what our hearts longed for. And we were yet still years from realizing that in some cases we weren't built for achieving our dream (I realized about my junior year of high school that I was too short and too slow to play professional basketball. The dreamer is always the last to know).

Eventually we started to let our dreams die. People began to tell us that we couldn't do the things we wanted. It was impossible. Responsible people don't pursue their dreams. Settle down, get a job, and be dependable. Take care of business, live the mundane, be content. Do you know what I say to that? Hooey! It is time to dream again! Why? Here are just a few reasons:

Avoiding regret. The facts are in, and some day we will all lie on our deathbed looking back through the history of our lives. We will undoubtedly think about what we wished we had done or accomplished. I, for one, don't want to regret what could have been, what should have been. So I am deciding today to pursue my dreams.

Making the world a better place. All of the great accomplishments that have ever happened began with a person who had a dream. Somebody rebuffed the nay-sayers and said to himself or herself, "This can be done, and I am the one who will do it." And in many instances they changed the world for the better. It isn't just the Martin Luther Kings and the J.F.K's either. Think of all the people we have never heard of, who have started things large and small that help people world-wide every day.

The world needs people like you to dream of something great and then to pursue it with all of your heart. Maybe you belong to a business, school, or organization that started out with good intentions but has settled into the same ol' same ol'. Shake them up and remind them of how they could really help people if only they would dream!

Personal and family fulfillment. One of the things that happens when we stop pursuing our dreams is that a little piece of us dies and we become disheartened, if only in that area of our lives. Stepping up and pursuing your dream rekindles that passion and zeal that everyone has the capacity for and lets us experience fulfillment. Having a purpose puts the zip in our step and the zing in our emotions!

Leaving a legacy. How will your children remember you? As one who sought all that life had to offer, using your gifts and talents to their fullest extent, leading the family with a zest for life, or as an overweight couch potato who could have been? Our children need to see that we dream; that we search for something better. They, in turn will do the same!

Big Dreams - Big Rewards

I talk a lot about dreams, if you haven't noticed! That's because I believe every single person has a dream inside of them just waiting to be turned loose! Each man and woman has a desire to do something great, to achieve excellence or to go somewhere wonderful. Most of the time these dreams have been hidden or forced inside because of fear. Many times these dreams have been put on the back burner to simmer while a "normal" life goes on.

I am on a one-man mission to destroy the concept of keeping dreams inside and to yourself! I want to motivate as many people as possible to passionately pursue their dreams and watch them come to fulfillment!

But what would you get out of dreaming big, you ask? The rewards are almost endless! But to get you started, here are a few of the top rewards you reap when you dream big!

A renewed passion for life and work. Feeling tired? Got the doldrums for life or work? There is a good reason – you aren't dreaming big enough! Get a big dream going and you will see your entire life revitalized and filled to overflowing with exuberant passion for life! Start today. Dream a big dream. Put it on the wall and start aiming for it. Live for it and you will see your energy level skyrocket!

Order will come to your life. A big dream serves as a focusing point. A focusing point will serve to bring order into your life. You will plot out a plan, lay out a strategy for reaching your dream. Since you will be so energized to reach your dream, and since you will have a plan for doing so, you will focus and discipline yourself in ways you never imagined possible before. You will see a new level of order emerge.

A life that ends the way you want it to. There will come a day when you will be reflecting back on a long life. What joy you will have to be able to be there that day with absolutely no regrets. Your life will end the way you want it to: Having pursued and achieved your big dreams!

A deep sense of personal fulfillment and satisfaction. As you live life there is one thing that hounds the dreamless: A lack of fulfillment. You see, I believe we were specifically designed to have big dreams, to pursue visions of greatness. And if we aren't doing so, we will see a certain lack of fulfillment. But when we do pursue those dreams – watch out because you will see an incredible sense of self-fulfillment wash over you like a tidal wave!

An ability to see others' lives changed for the better. Big dreams will give you the opportunity to stand back and know that you have helped others grow, achieve more and experience the best. If you haven't helped others, then your dream was too small because a big dream is by definition one that helps others as well.

I want you to experience the above rewards and the good news is that you can! You can see your dreams become reality and you can see your rewards multiply!

Here is a checklist to get you going:

- Do you have an identified dream?
- Have you laid out a plan for reaching it?
- Have you taken a first step to do so?
- What is the next step you need to take to reach your dream?
- What are the rewards you are experiencing right now?

<u>Seven Steps to Achieving Your Dream</u>

"Vision is the spectacular that inspires us to carry out the mundane."
--Chris Widener

Can achievement be broken down into steps? Well, it isn't always that clean and easy, but I do know that those who achieve great things usually go through much of the same process, with many of the items listed below as part of that process. So if you have been struggling with achievement, look through the following and internalize the thoughts presented. Then begin to apply them. You will be on the road to achieving your dream!

1. Dream it - Everything begins in the heart and mind. Every great achievement began in the mind of one person. They dared to dream, to believe that it was possible. Take some time to allow yourself to ask "What if?" Think big. Don't let negative thinking discourage you. You want to be a "dreamer." Dream of the possibilities for yourself, your family, and for others. If you had a dream that you let grow cold, re-ignite the dream! Fan the flames. Life is too short to let it go. (Also, check out my article "Dare to Dream Again," which has been read by close to a million people. You can see it at the website – www.madeforsuccess.com)

2. Believe it - Yes, your dream needs to be big. It needs to be something that is seemingly beyond your capabilities. But it also must be believable. You must be able to say that if certain things take place, if others help, if you work hard enough, though it is a big dream, it can still be done. Good example: A person with no college education can dream that he will build a 50 million-dollar a year company. That is big, but believable. Bad example: That a 90 year-old woman with arthritis will someday run a marathon in under 3 hours. It is big all right, but also impossible. She should instead focus on building a 50 million-dollar a year business! And she better get a move on!

3. See it - The great achievers have a habit. They "see" things. They picture themselves walking around their CEO office in their new 25 million-dollar corporate headquarters, even while they are sitting on a folding chair in their garage "headquarters." Great free-throw shooters in the NBA picture the ball going through the basket. PGA golfers picture the ball going straight down the fairway. World-class speakers picture themselves speaking with energy and emotion. All of this grooms the mind to control the body to carry out the dream.

4. Tell it - One reason many dreams never go anywhere is because the dreamer keeps it all to himself. It is a quiet dream that only lives inside of his mind. The one who wants to achieve their dream must tell that dream to many people. One reason: As we continually say it, we begin to believe it more and more. If we are talking about it then it must be possible. Another reason: It holds us accountable. When we have told others, it spurs us on to actually do it so we don't look foolish.

5. Plan it - Every dream must take the form of a plan. The old saying that you "get what you plan for" is so true. Your dream won't just happen. You need to sit down, on a regular basis, and plan out your strategy for achieving the dream. Think through all of the details. Break the whole plan down into small, workable parts. Then set a time frame for accomplishing each task on your "dream plan."

6. Work it - Boy, wouldn't life be grand if we could quit before this one! Unfortunately, the successful are usually the hardest workers. While the rest of the world is sitting on their couch watching re-runs of Gilligan's Island, achievers are working on their goal, achieving their dream. I have an equation that I work with: Your short-term tasks, multiplied by time, equal your long-term accomplishments. If you work on it each day, eventually you will achieve your dream. War and Peace was written in longhand, page by page.

> *To bring one's self to a frame of mind and to the proper energy to accomplish things that require plain hard work continuously is the one big battle that everyone has. When this battle is won for all time, then everything is easy.*
>
> *Thomas A. Buckner*

7. Enjoy it - When you have reached your goal and you are living your dream, be sure to enjoy it. In fact, enjoy the trip, too. Give yourself some rewards along the way. Give yourself a huge reward when you get there. Help others enjoy it. Be gracious and generous. Use your dream to better others. Then go back to number 1. And dream a little bigger this time!

Live the Life
Principle Number Two:
VISION IS THE CORNERSTONE

Stop Just Writing About Your Past and Start Writing Your Future!

"The history of free men is never written by chance, but by choice – their choice." Dwight D. Eisenhower.

Many people spend a lot of time on their history. Some do it purposefully with such hobbies as journaling, while others simply write and rewrite their history over and over in their minds. Depending upon the way you go about this, this can be good or bad. If you are doing it so you can reflect back on your life, that's good. If you are doing it so you can learn from your past, that's good too. Unfortunately, many people do it simply as a subconscious act of running themselves into the ground over and over.

What you "write" in your mind is an act of mental discipline, just as what you write on a sheet of paper is a discipline. Keep that in mind.

So if this is true, that we can make a choice as to what we want to write, both literally and figuratively, we have an extraordinary opportunity!

Instead of going over and over our past, we can choose to write our future! Have you ever thought about writing your future before it even happens to you? Well now you can – and you will!

Here is a process that will let you determine and write your own future!

Choose to choose your own future. If you don't make the decision to accept responsibility for your own future, then you are choosing to not write your future. You must choose to choose. Do you?

Determine what you want your future to be. Be specific.

What do you want to earn?

Where do you want to live?

What do you want to weigh?

What do you want to do for a living?

What do you want to do in your leisure time?

> *We acquire the strength we have overcome.*
>
> *Ralph Waldo Emerson*

How much do you want to retire on?

If you don't know the answers to these questions, then you may as well not even begin to write your future. Take some time to answer them fully.

Get a good understanding of your strengths and weaknesses. If you are going to write your future, you will have to have a sober understanding of what you are good at and what you are not particularly good at. Maybe ask a

34

good friend or your spouse to give you an honest appraisal of your strengths and weaknesses.

Focus on playing to your strengths while ever improving your weaknesses. Be sure that what you are doing is utilizing your strengths to their fullest. And you don't want to forget your weaknesses, even while you are trying to stay away from them. Instead, set smaller goals for improvement in your areas of weakness while you set grand goals for the areas you are strongest in!

Get out a three pieces of paper. On the top of one, write, "One year from today I will…" On the next write, "Three years from today I will…" On the last write, "Ten years from today I will…" Then begin to fill them out. Make commitments to yourself. As you write them, end each sentence with a transition to how you are going to do it. For example, you may write, "One year from today I will… Have $4800 in my saving account by saving $400 per month."

Start putting only information into your mind that will benefit the fulfillment of the kind of life you are writing about. For example, if you have a hard time spending money rather than saving it, you should probably cancel all of the catalogues that come each day that entice you to spend. Instead, spend the time you would have spent thumbing through catalogues going through financial growth material instead.

Discipline yourself to spend your time in a manner that will help you get to your goals. For example, cut out five hours of television a week and spend that time on your goals instead. That would be a difference of 260 hours in the next year! Wow! What could you do with another 260 hours? Almost anything!

You do not have to be a paper cup blowing to and fro in the wind! You do not have to live at the whims of other people or circumstances. You CAN choose your future! You can write it out just the way you want it to happen! Yes, ups and downs will come but you will outlast them and eventually arrive at your destiny. Then, when you get to the end of your life, you will know how it all turns out because you will have been the author!

Get going – write your own future!

Your Date with Destiny

Destiny. What a powerful word. And the great thing about it? Everyone has one! You have a destiny! Another great thing about destiny? We have a significant role in shaping our own destiny! In essence, you can choose your date with destiny – powerful!
Your destiny is the dream that lies within you of your desired and preferred future. And the things that we choose each day are what lead us to that destiny: Our actions, our words, our attitudes, and our relationships. They all add up to develop and shape that date on which we will reach our destiny.

Here are some thoughts to think about as you work on shaping your Date with Destiny:

The Mental Question: Do you believe that you can achieve a life of abundance? The frank truth is that many people simply do not believe that they can achieve what lies in their heart. Success is for someone else, a better person, or a smarter person. This is not true and is perhaps the greatest obstacle we face on the journey to our destiny. If we are to achieve abundance in life, we must first believe we can, or face our own continual self-sabotage of what a college professor of mine called "stinkin'-thinkin'."

Here is the truth:

It doesn't matter what your intelligence is.

It doesn't matter what your current resources are.

It doesn't matter what you currently earn.

It doesn't matter what family you came from.

Nothing in your current circumstances matters in whether or not you can achieve your destiny! Nothing! Now, your current state may make it a longer or harder journey than someone else, but the possibility is always there no matter what your current circumstances are.

And that is the message we need to continually tell ourselves. "I can do it." Not "I can't do it."

Clear vision. Do you have one of your destiny? Here are some questions to determine whether or not your vision is clear.

Can you describe it in intricate detail?

Can you "see" it?
Can you "feel" it?
Can you "hear" it?

Here are a couple of illustrations.

Perhaps you came from a dysfunctional family and your dream is to have great moments with your family.

Let's start with a Thanksgiving meal. Can you see each person there? What are they wearing? Are they smiling? What is the conversation? Can you hear the laughter? Can you experience the joy? Can you smell the turkey? Can you see people hugging each other and saying "This was wonderful," as they leave?

> *It's not what's happening to you now or what has happened in your past that determines who you become. Rather, it's your decisions about what to focus on, what things mean to you, and what you're going to do about them that will determine your ultimate destiny.*
>
> *Anthony Robbins*

Another scenario: Your company. Can you see the large building you are in? Can you see the workers? Can you feel the positive attitude they have as they carry out their work? Can you experience the excitement as you get the quarterly results? Can you see yourself handing out healthy bonuses that bring pleasant surprises to your employees?

This is where it begins. A clear vision of your destiny.

Consider your resources. Are you aware of the resources you will need in order to set your date with destiny? Do you know how you will go about getting them?

What are the natural gifts and talents that you have? How can you best utilize them in achieving your destiny?

What are your current levels of resources?

Money?

Time?

Emotional health?

Help from others such as friends, family, employees or volunteers?

What will be your needed future level of resources? And have you developed a plan to achieve this level?

The last thing I want you to do is to fix a date in the future that you will be living your destiny by. A real date. This enables you to begin to work backwards in setting goals to move you along the way, providing you with future points to strive for and evaluation points to reflect upon.

Here are the points again:

- Answer the mental question: Do I really believe?
- Develop a clear vision.
- Consider the resources needed.
- Set a date with destiny.
- Develop a plan to get there.

Re-Developing Your Vision

One of the most important things we can do for our businesses, schools, and organizations is to have vision. Vision is a clear picture of a desired end result that you are aiming for.

However, sometimes, no matter how big our vision was originally, we find ourselves focusing in on the daily events that require our attention but have nothing or little to do with our ultimate vision.

Occasionally, we think to ourselves, "Hey, I'm not really getting any closer to my vision. I'm spinning my wheels here." This is when it is time to re-develop your vision!
Here are some helpful hints in doing just that.

Re-evaluate your original vision. Maybe your original dream wasn't realistic according to your strengths, your abilities, or your circumstances. Maybe it is time to change or modify the vision to make it attainable.

Assess your strengths. To achieve your vision, you and your staff will have to operate out of your strengths. If you are having a hard time moving toward your current vision, perhaps it is because the vision requires extended application of strengths that you and/or your organization don't have. Either you need to hire into those strengths, develop those strengths, or re-develop the vision.

Ask yourself where your passions lie. If we are to attain great things, they must be aligned with those things that burn deep within us. Do you still have a passion for your vision? Does your staff have a passion for your vision? If not, you need to develop the passion, or find the vision that you can pour your passion into. Never underestimate the power of passion and excitement in moving you toward (or keeping you from) your vision.

Ask yourself what it is that you value. What is important to you? How will fulfilling my current vision, fulfill my desire to do something important and worthwhile for myself, my family, my employees, and my community?

Break the vision down into easy-to-achieve steps. This helps us see that the vision is attainable. It lets us know the end result, but focus intently on achieving the next goal. This, step-by-step, moves us toward the vision.

Live the Life
Principle Number Three:
GOALS ARE FOR ACHIEVING

Get Your Goals – Guaranteed!

"Goals" is a topic that many people talk about, both in a positive as well as a negative sense. Some people are goal maniacs and others think they are a waste of time. Me? I am somewhat different. I just care about one thing – results. Goals: write 'em down; don't write 'em down, I don't care. Just get them! Achieve them! Live them! That is the only thing that should matter about goals, right?

If the only thing that matters is that we achieve our goals, then let's talk about ways that will guarantee that we get our goals! There is such a way… and here it is:

First, be realistic. Too many people get hyped up by people promising them the world and they set goals that simply aren't realistic. Then they are disappointed and then decide that "goals" are bad. But wait a minute. Don't I teach that anybody can achieve anything? Sort of. We have to be realistic. The best example is that a seven-foot center who plays basketball will never be a world champion jockey. A person who is five feet, two inches could be, given time. This is the difference between a realistic goal and one that isn't. Take some time and set a realistic goal or goals. This will make your goals guaranteed from the get go!

Second, memorize your goals. Set them in stone in your mind. Know what they are. Prioritize them in order of importance and memorize them so that if anyone asked you, "What are your top seven goals?" you could answer immediately. This will embed the goals and the desired outcomes into your mind, which is the seed of action.

> *If you don't know where you are going, you might wind up someplace else.*
>
> *Yogi Berra*

 Visualize your goals. Some people are really into this. Some people think it is total hooey. I am in the middle. I do not think that there is anything "magical" about the visualization process, but I do think that taking some time to regularly envision your dream and goals is a great thing. It deepens your desire to get your goals. It puts you into a frame of mind where you operate in a peak state. So, don't overdo it, but don't throw the baby out with the bathwater either. Plant your goals deep into your mind by visualizing them periodically.

 Set time frames. Don't let your goal be, "I want to lose twenty pounds." Instead, let it be, "I want to lose twenty pounds in four months." Again, a reminder to be realistic. But you can do wonders for your goal setting if you break down your goals and put time frames on them. This gives it a sense of urgency. It makes it something you are working "toward" rather than working "on." In fact, I would suggest setting long-range time frames, mid-range time frames, and short-range time frames.

 Spend time and money on your goals. Realize that any goal worth achieving is worth spending your resources on, specifically time and money. Buy books, go to seminars, join associations, hire a coach, etc.--whatever you need to do to get your goals! Spending time and money will seed your dreams and you will reap the end result far beyond what you put into it. Big dreams have big costs, but even little dreams have a cost associated with them, so count the cost.

Surround yourself with people who can propel you to your goals. Never underestimate the power of the people around you to either drag you down or lift you up. Poisonous people can destroy your goal by systematically draining you of your passion and desire and replacing it with total pessimism! Passionate and positive people can invigorate you with renewed energy and a mind set on the dream. Be around people who will energize you!

Act on your goals each and every day. Even if it is just a small step, it will leave you closer to your goal each and every day. If you have a savings goal, set aside even one dollar a day. Take a jar and empty your change into it at the end of each day. If you

> *Our goals can only be reached through a vehicle of a plan, in which we must fervently believe, and upon which we must vigorously act. There is no other route to success.*
>
> *Stephen A. Brennan*

want to write a book, write each day, if even just two paragraphs! Small, step-by-step actions will produce the goal – guaranteed!

Be persistent! I have long said that if the three most important words in real estate are "location, location, location," then the three most important words in getting what you desire are "persistence, persistence, persistence." In fact, be tenaciously persistent. Be ruthlessly persistent.

Look, there will be all sorts of barriers and obstacles you will have to overcome if you want to achieve your dream. Dreams don't just roll over and die. You have to attack them! Go for it and don't give up! They can, and will, be yours!

Can you get your goals – guaranteed? You bet you can. And you will, if you put into practice the above principles.

If you…

Are realistic.

Memorize your goals.

Visualize your goals.

Set time frames.

Spend time and money on your goals.

Surround yourself with positive people.

Act on your goals every day and…

Be persistent.

You can get your goals – guaranteed!

Simple Ways to Super-Charge Your Goals and Make Them Work!

Goals. Most people have a love-hate relationship with goals. They love them because they are such a great idea and a wonderful way to motivate us to achieve, as well as evaluate our progress, but hate them because for many, they more often than not go unattained and simply frustrate them. This isn't what goals should do!

So I thought I would list some simple ways to set goals so that we achieve them! After all, what good is a goal if it isn't something you achieve? Here are some simple steps you can take to make sure that you see change in your life this year.

Narrow your focus. That's right, start small. Pick two or three areas--tops--that you want to work on. Too many people say to themselves, "I want to do this, and this, and this, and this......" and they end up doing nothing! Most of what you do throughout your day can be done without a lot of mental or emotional exertion, but change isn't one of them. So focus on a couple, to begin. This way you can get some victory in these areas. Here are some areas to think about: Physical, Intellectual, Emotional, Spiritual, Financial, and Relational.

> *You must have long term goals to keep you from being frustrated by short-term failures.*
>
> *Charles C. Noble*

What areas need some work? Now, what one thing should be the first item on the change list? The others will come later, but for now, you should focus on two or three.

Keep the long-term in mind, but set your sights on achieving your goals in the short-term. Do you want to lose 75 pounds? Good. Long-term you will. But for now, think short-term. Don't think about losing 75 pounds in eighteen months. Think about losing 5 pounds in one month. This does two things. First, It makes it urgent. Instead of blowing it and saying, "Oh well, I still have 17 months to lose the 75 pounds," (because eventually that becomes 2 months to lose 75 pounds) your goal is only a few weeks out. This is better in terms of reaching your long-term goal. Secondly, as you reach these shorter goals, it gives you regular victories instead of regular progress. Progress feels good, but achieving a goal is awesome!

Reward yourself when you achieve the goal. When you lose the 5 pounds in a month, go get yourself a milkshake. But just one! Then get back to your goal for the next month. This puts a little fun back into the process of self-control and self-discipline. You will look forward to the reward and when the going gets tough, you will say, "two more weeks, two more pounds, then…"

That's it. I truly believe that it can be that simple for you.

This adds some ideas to the above.

1. Don't bite off more than you can chew. Instead of saying, "I am going to quit my three-pack-a-day habit cold turkey," say "I am going to drop to a pack and a half a day." You can always make new resolutions when you have achieved the first ones. Give yourself small victories a little at a time. Instead of saying "I am going to lose 75 pounds," say "I am going to lose 20 pounds."

2. Be specific in your timeline. Don't just say, "I am going to lose 20 pounds." Say, "I am going to lose 20 pounds by April 1st." This way, when you start to be tempted in the ice cream aisle in the middle of February, you can say, "Nope, only 10 more pounds to go in a month and a half, and I am not going to blow it."

3. Post your resolutions where you will see them every day. This will keep the resolution in the front of your mind at all times. Instead of forgetting that you are trying to lose weight and ordering a big, thick porterhouse, you will have been reminded earlier that day that you need to go with something a little more on the lighter side. It will help your will beat your desire.

4. Find an encouraging person, who you respect, to keep you accountable. This person should ask you, at an interval established by the both of you, how it is going. They must be the encouraging type, though. If you are blowing it, they can say, "Well, that's okay, get back to it tomorrow." If you are doing well, they can say, "Awesome job. I'll talk to you next week." You will look forward to their weekly encouragement.

5. Find a partner. That's right, someone who is trying to accomplish the same thing (or something different if need be). Just make sure that they really want to change, or they will end up just bellyaching about how hard it is, and you could both fall into the abyss.

6. Write down a list of all of the benefits that will come if you accomplish this. If it is losing weight it might be something like this: Feel better, better self-esteem, longer life, clothes are more comfortable, no more time spent sewing on popped buttons, wife says you look 22 again, etc. If it is quitting smoking, it may look like this: Better breath, no more brown fingers, no more wrinkles on my face, no more red eyes, no more smelly clothes, longer life, wife won't make me spend two hours a day on the back porch, etc. This will help you see what you will get from accomplishing your resolution.

7. Plan a reward if you accomplish your resolution. It can be anything from small to large. If you drop the twenty pounds, go out for dinner and dessert. Then get back to lose the next 20. If it is quitting smoking, go on a mini-vacation. Whatever you do, reward yourself, or let a spouse or a friend pick the reward. Then splurge and enjoy!

Make Greatness Your Goal!

If greatness is your goal, whether in your business life, your personal relationships or your own personal growth, here are some guidelines to get you on your way. Greatness is possible! You can achieve the goals you set for yourself, and you can make a difference in your own life and those who live and work around you! Set greatness as your goal! Here's how:

Identify greatness for yourself. While there are some basic generalities that most people would consider great, there are broader definitions of greatness, ones that each individual sets for him or herself. For example, most people would consider Mother Theresa great,

> *No great man lives in vain. The history of the world is but the biography of great men.*
>
> *Thomas Carlyle*

while only some would consider Donald Trump great. Helping humanity is a broad generality while building a real estate fortune isn't. So what you need to first do is ask, "What does greatness look like for this company, organization, family or for myself?" From there you can develop values and a mission statement, etc. But if you don't first identify it, you'll never reach it.

Maximize targeted end results. As Covey says, "begin with the end in mind." What end results do you want? Be specific. Come up with all of them. Maximize them. Leave no stone unturned. Set out for yourself all of the goals or end results you must hit in order to reach greatness. Write them down, memorize them and distribute them broadly (if doing this for a group). Maximize your targeted end results!

Make distinction your endeavor. What is the endeavor of the great? Usually, it is to distinguish themselves from the average. They seek to rise above the rest by the quality of their product or service. Everything goes toward the goal of making

> *Greatness does not approach him who is forever looking down.*
>
> *Hitopadesa*

themselves distinct from the run of the mill. That is their mission. And in doing so, they make themselves great!

Map your effort thoroughly. The three most important words in real estate are "location, location, location." In reaching a goal, the three most important words are "plan, plan, plan." Okay, "execute" and "persevere" work too, but go with me here! Too many people wish they would achieve something, but they never write down a plan for getting there. When I want to go on a long trip, I don't just wish to get there. I plan on how to get there. I get a map, I figure out distances, times, etc. Map out your goal thoroughly. This will help you achieve greatness.

Regularly take time for regeneration. Achieving greatness is hard! You will care more, work harder, and take more lumps and setbacks than the rest. So you will need to take time to regenerate so you can fight again another day. Your body needs rest. Your mind needs rest. Your emotions need rest. Your spirit needs rest. I firmly believe that a person who rests well can do more in less time than the one who works without setting aside time for regeneration. You may be able to reach goals without rest, but somewhere along the line, you will fall harder and longer if you aren't regularly regenerating yourself. So take your vacation time this year!

Have a strict evaluation process. Every plan and goal needs an evaluation tool. And it should be a strict evaluation process. This is how you objectively decide whether or not you are proceeding toward your goal. If you have the right evaluation tool and you look six months into it and you aren't hitting the goals, perhaps you need to change the goal or the way you are going after it. The evaluation process is not to be underestimated in its importance!

Take somebody else with you. True greatness is not individual. The one who becomes great spreads the reward of greatness around. Incorporate many people into the plan and let them eat of the fruit of success. I live in an area that has literally thousands of millionaires created by a company that had a vision of greatness. And while yes, they experience the reward, the rewards then go out many levels through the whole community, from businesses that support our community to non-profit groups, churches, and schools. True greatness blesses those many levels away.

Learn to party! Party? Yes! What good is greatness if you can't enjoy it? And not just the final destination but also the entire journey. Be sure to stop along the way and relish in your movement. Celebrate small and large victories. This keeps the sprit high and the big momentum rolling! Spend the money, buy the food and blow up the balloons – it's time to celebrate!

Live the Life
Principle Number Four:
THE TENACIOUS BIRD GETS THE WORM

Take a Turn at Tenacious!

"Nothing in this world can take the place of persistence. Talent will not; nothing is more common than unsuccessful people with talent. Genius will not; unrewarded genius is almost a proverb. Education will not; the world is full of educated derelicts. Persistence and determination alone are omnipotent. The slogan 'press on' has solved and always will solve the problems of the human race."   --Calvin Coolidge

I have worked with many successful people; people who have achieved the kinds of lives they have dreamed about. I have also worked with many people who are not anywhere near where they want to be in life. Many times those who are not successful resent those who are and believe that somehow success was handed to those who have achieved much.

> *You become a champion by fighting one more round. When things are tough, you fight one more round.*
>
> *James J. Corbett*

What I have found however is that actually the reverse is true. Those who have achieved much have worked much HARDER than those who are not successful.

You wouldn't believe the stories of struggle that I hear from those who now appear on "top of the heap." Yes, they are successful; but no, it wasn't handed to them! And I find that most of the unsuccessful people who come to me actually haven't been tenacious at all. I find that with many of the people I speak to who complain about their lack of success simply haven't persevered and been tenacious. When I ask them questions I usually get excuses. Yes, there are exceptions on both sides, but I find this to be almost universally true.

If you are one who finds yourself dreaming of a better life, or looking at someone who "has it made," I would ask you to take a long, deep look inward and at your life to find whether or not you have actually been tenacious in pursuit of your dreams. How long have you been trying? Many people who achieve much go for YEARS before they achieve what their hearts long for. How hard have you tried? Most people who achieve much have given up much. They have sacrificed much. They strive valiantly for what it is that resides deep in their dreams. They just plain ol' work hard!

So what are the principles of tenacity? What do you need to know in order to take your turn at the tenacious? Here are some thoughts to start your fire and get you going!

1. Sometimes you just have to outlast the others.

"Success seems to be largely a matter of hanging on after others have let go." William Feather

I have found that many people start on their dreams, but most never finish. Then those who stop resent those who make it. The truth is that most people who become successful have simply mastered the art of "keeping on keeping on"! I myself can remember early on in my career when I would get discouraged and I literally said to myself, "One more week. Just give it one more week." Quite frankly, this is what got me through a couple of years of my work early on. I hung on as others let go.

It is easy to get disheartened. Ask those who have achieved success if they ever got disheartened, and you will find some of the most amazing stories you have ever heard. Give it a try: Go to the most successful person you know and ask them if they ever thought about quitting. Ask them how they kept on going. You will be amazed at what you hear.

> *Determine what specific goal you want to achieve. Then dedicate yourself to its attainment with unswerving singleness of purpose, the trenchant zeal of a crusader.*
>
> *Paul J. Meyer*

2. Sometimes you just have to hold on at the end.

"When you get to the end of your rope, tie a knot and hang on." Franklin Roosevelt

I wonder how many people have quit just as they would have begun their entrance into success. Sure there are many who quit at the first sign of hard work, but what about those who, after the tenth time of trial then give up, just as fate would have seen them go through one last hurdle and then into the promised land? How many people were on their last hurdle and decided not to jump? How many people had just one more mountain pass to go? Or just one more river to cross?

Of course we will never know, but certainly some of the people who quit are doing so on what would have been their last trial, right?

So what does this mean for you? For me it means I do not quit because I would hate to find out later that all I needed was just one last effort and I would have achieved my goal. What if it isn't my last trial? That's okay because as long as I keep going, eventually I will get to my last trial, I will overcome it, and I will enter the Winner's Circle.

> *We can do anything we want to do if we stick to it long enough.*
>
> *Helen Keller*

3. Sometimes the most beautiful results come from dull things under pressure.

"Diamonds are nothing more than chunks of coal that stuck to their jobs." Malcolm Forbes

If coal wasn't an inanimate object it would certainly scream, "Stop! I want out!" But that coal, when facing incredible pressure, is turned into one of earth's most precious possessions. Ugly, dirty old coal is transformed into beautiful diamonds.

Instead of looking at pressure and trials as the reason to quit, get tenacious and see them as the very thing that will make your life the beautiful thing that you desire it to be. See it as your opportunity to learn, to grow, and to be transformed. See these trials as the very things that will enable you to have the life you dream of!

Trials will surely come. Life will get hard. You will want to quit.

58

Then you will have a choice: Will you give up? Or will you take your turn at tenacious. The choice you make will determine much of the rest of your life.

My advice? Take your turn at tenacious. You will become stronger, and you will end up living the life you dream of!

My Top Four Pointers for Kicking Your Life Into High Gear

How would you like to kick your life into high gear? I can help you! Your life doesn't have to be stale and full of drudgery. Your life can be lived at the highest levels, experiencing joy in every area! I want to give you my top pointers for kicking your life into high gear so you can get moving on the fast track to success!

But first... A secret key to understanding success.

Secret Key: Success isn't just doing certain things, though we will certainly do certain things to become a certain kind of person. What kind of person you are is what determines your success in life. Yes, you can do right things and achieve a certain level of success, but not the kind of success I am talking about – true-life success.

So what are my four tips? Here they are:

1. Become a person of Vision.

Vision is the spectacular that causes us to carry out the mundane. Vision is what sees us

The only limits are, as always, those of vision.

James Broughton

59

through the dark days so we do not give up and settle for second best. Vision is the grand scheme that we relentlessly pursue. Vision is the goal we aim for. The best way to kick your life into high gear and begin to succeed in what you want to succeed in is to begin to become a person of vision.

The successful person has a fully developed vision of their destination. So let me ask you a simple question:

Do YOU know where you are going?

And not only do you have a vision of where you are going, but is your vision fully developed? Now certainly we cannot know everything that will happen to us in the future, but we can develop the plan fully, allowing in our plan for a variety of contingency plans. "But Chris, that is a lot of work." It is, but when you look across the board at people who have succeeded much, they are people who laid out most of their life and work before it happened. Life didn't just happen to them. They didn't just stumble into success. They planned for it and they created it.

The Tests of Vision

Is it Clear?

Is it Concise?

Is it Inspiring?

Is it Achievable?

Is it Easy to Memorize?

Ask your self the questions above and let the answers begin to shape the vision you have for your life.

The tighter and clearer the vision you have for your life, the sooner you will kick your life into high gear!

2. Become a person of Passion.

Passion. Mmmmm…. Passion. Passion is the burning of the heart. It is the unbridled running amuck of the emotions. It is the overwhelming desire to accomplish your goal. It transcends the mental assent to a set of ideals. It drives and thrusts you toward your goal. You MUST have it!

Those who consider themselves intellectuals will underestimate the power of passion. The fact is that the victory isn't only in the mind. The truths of the mind

> *Nothing is so intolerable to man as being fully at rest, without a passion.*
>
> *Blaise Pascal*

are driven by the passion of the heart. So by all means, fuel the passion for life that resides deep within your soul.

Passion is like a fire. It can rage or it can smolder. Even if all you have is barely lit embers, you can fan into flame the fire of your passion for life, love, and the goals and vision you have for your life! Commit yourself to becoming a person who lives passionately!

3. Become a person of Priorities.

As I have worked through the years with people who achieve much and have lives that are constantly in high gear, I notice something amazing about them: They are people with an extraordinary ability to know the right thing to do and to actually do it in a timely fashion.

For example, a friend of mine was in charge of a three-day event a few weeks ago that was attended by close to 250,000 people and was featured on national and international television. Four days before the event he told me he had nothing to do and felt guilty. I encouraged him by reminding him that this was actually a sign of his incredible ability to have focused on and lived out his priorities throughout the whole year before the event took place.

When all was said and done, living and working out of his priorities enabled him to kick back and enjoy the fruit of his (and hundreds of his employees) labor. His

> *It is the mark of great people to treat trifles as trifles and important matters as important.*
>
> *Doris Lessing*

life was in high gear and because he is a person of priorities, he is enjoying life. You can too.

Discern the important things that you must involve yourself in to have the life you want. Then relentlessly live out of those priorities. Say "no" to everything else!

4. Become a person of Excellence.

People who live life in high gear, succeeding in every area of life, are people who place a high emphasis on, and strive for, excellence in every area of life. Good just won't do. The best is the target.

Even when they fail or do poorly, they make an inner commitment to do an excellent job the next time. They are people who want, and live for excellence in their work, their play, their finances, their relationships – everything!

Do you long for a life lived in high gear? One that is filled with joy and achievement? It is possible! Give some time to contemplate how you can make changes in the next

> *He who has put a good finish to his undertaking is said to have placed a golden crown to the whole.*
>
> *Eustachius*

few days and weeks in the following areas and see if your life doesn't kick into high gear!

- Vision
- Passion
- Priorities
- Excellence

They are yours for the taking! Go get 'em!

Live the Life
Principle Number Five:
STAY MOTIVATED FOR SUCCESS

The Top Six Ways to Stay Motivated

I receive many emails from people that ask basically the same question: How can I keep myself motivated long term? This seems to be quite a common dilemma for many people, so I want to address it because it can be done! Here are my tips for staying motivated:

1. Get motivated every day. Zig Ziglar was once confronted about being a "motivational speaker." The guy said to him, "You guys come and get people hyped up and then you leave and the motivation goes away. It doesn't last, and then you have to get motivated again." Zig reminded the gentleman that baths are the same way, but we think it is a good idea to take a bath every day!

It is true that motivation doesn't last. We have to renew it each and every day. That is okay. It doesn't make motivation a bad thing. We simply have to realize that if we want to stay motivated over the long term, it is something we will have to apply ourselves to each and every day.

> *If it doesn't come from within, it doesn't come.*
>
> *Herman Cain*

2. **Have a vision for your life.** The root word of motivation is "motive." The definition of motive is, "A reason to act." This is the cognitive or rational side of motivation. It is your vision. You have to have a vision that is big enough to motivate you. If you are making $50,000 a year, it isn't going to motivate you to set your goal at $52,000 a year. You just won't get motivated for that because the reward isn't enough. Maybe $70,000 a year would work for you. Set out a vision and a strategy for getting there. Have a plan and work the plan.

3. **Fuel your passion.** Much of motivation is emotional. I don't know quite how it works, but I do know THAT it works. Emotion is a powerful force in getting us going. Passion is an emotion, so fuel your passion. "Well, I like to work on logic," you may say. Great, now work on your passion. Set yourself on a course to have a consuming desire for your goal, whatever it is. Do whatever you can to feel the emotion and use it to your advantage!

4. **Work hard enough to get results.** You can build on your motivation by getting results. The harder you work, the more results you will get and the more results you get, the more you will be

> *Motivation is what gets you started. Habit is what keeps you going.*
>
> *Jim Ryun*

motivated to get more. These things all build on one another. If you want to lose weight, then lose the first few pounds. When the belt moves to the next notch you will get fired up to get it to the notch beyond that!

5. **Put good materials into your mind.** I can't say this enough – listen to tapes. I still listen to tapes regularly. I buy tape clubs from other speakers, and I learn and grow.

Their successes motivate me to attain my own successes! Read good books. Read books that teach you new ideas and skills. Read books that tell the stories of successful people. Buy them, read them, and get motivated! Buy great music and listen to it. I just did a cycling class at the health club today. Whenever a good song came on I was actually able to get motivated to ride faster! It gets you going and motivates you!

6. Ride the momentum when it comes. Sometimes you will just be clicking and sometimes you won't. That is okay. It is the cycle of life. When you aren't clicking, plug away. When you are clicking, pour it on because momentum will help you get larger gains in a shorter period of time with less energy. That is the Momentum Equation! When you are feeling good about how your work is going, ride the momentum and get as much out of it as you can!

These are the top six ways to stay motivated:

- Get motivated every day.
- Have a vision for your life.
- Fuel your passion.
- Work hard enough to get results.
- Put good materials into your mind.
- Ride the momentum when it comes.

These are simple principles, that when you put them to work regularly, will change your life by keeping you motivated all the time! Get going!

Finding Motivation: What To Do When You Don't Feel Like Doing Anything

"The measure of your success usually comes down to who wins the battle that rages between the two of you. The 'you' who wants to stop, give up, or take it easy, and the 'you' who chooses to beat back that which would stand in the way of your success - complacency." Chris Widener

In all of my interactions with people, I've never found anyone, regardless of their level of success, who doesn't sometimes find themselves simply not wanting to do the things that they need and want to do. It is a part of human nature that there will be times, in spite of all that we need to do and even desire to do, we will find ourselves not wanting to do anything. And what separates those who will become successful from those who will maintain the status-quo, is the ability at those very crucial moments of time when we are making decisions about what we will do, to choose to find the inner motivation that will enable us to conquer our complacency and move on in action.

I find that I confront this issue in my life on a regular basis, so the following success strategies are not merely pie in the sky techniques, but proven ways to get yourself to go even when you don't feel like doing anything.

Honestly evaluate whether or not you need a break. This is the first thing that I usually do when I find that I don't want to get to a specific action. Maybe we have been working very hard, and the lethargy we are feeling is really our body and emotions telling us that we simply need a break. And this is where it takes real intellectual honesty because when we don't need a break our mind is still telling us we need a break! But sometimes we do need a break.

I'll give you a good example. I don't particularly like to exercise, but I do almost every day. Sometimes, I find myself thinking about how I just didn't feel like going to the club that day. Most of the time I am just being lazy. However, sometimes I realize that my body needs a break. So from time to time I will take a one or two day break from working out. The benefits of this are two-fold: One, my body gets a break to regenerate itself. Two, after a day or two, I begin to miss my workout, and eagerly anticipate returning to the gym.

Other examples: Perhaps you are a salesman who has been phoning clients for a week straight, day and night. You wake up one morning and just don't feel like doing it anymore. Well, take a break for the morning. Go to a coffee shop and read the paper. Go to the driving range and hit some golf balls. Take a break and then get back to it!

> *What separates those who will become successful from those who will maintain the status quo is the ability to choose to find the inner motivation to conquer their complacency.*
>
> *Chris Widener*

Start small. I'm at a point in my workout schedule now where a typical workout day for me consists of 30 to 45 minutes of aerobic exercise, and about 30 minutes of weight lifting. So when I find myself not wanting to get up and go to the gym, I will sometimes make a commitment to go and just do a smaller workout. Instead of deciding not to go, I'll commit to doing 15 to 20 minutes of aerobic exercise and 15 to 30 minutes of weight lifting. This is also good for two reasons. One, I actually get some exercise that day. And two, it keeps me from getting into a cycle of giving up when I don't feel like moving toward action.

Other examples: Maybe you are a writer who simply doesn't want to write today. Instead of the long day writing you had planned, decide that you will at least outline a couple of new articles. You will at least get these done, and you may have found that you put yourself into the writing mood after all.

Change your routine. I have found that what keeps me in the best physical shape and burns the most calories for me, is to do 30 to 45 minutes on the treadmill every day. Now let me be very blunt. I find running on the treadmill to be extremely boring. Usually I can get myself to do it, but sometimes I need to vary my routine. So instead of 30 to 45 minutes on a treadmill, I will break down my aerobic exercise routine into a number of different areas. I will do 10 to 15 minutes on treadmills, 10 to 15 minutes on the reclining cycle, 5 to 10 minutes on the rowing machine, 5 to 10 minutes on the stair stepper, and then back on the treadmill for five to 10 minutes. I still get my exercise, but I'm a lot less bored.

Other examples: Maybe you are in construction and you have been working on the plumbing for a week, and it is getting monotonous. Don't do the plumbing today! Go frame-in the office.

Reward yourself. One way that I motivate myself to do something when I don't feel like doing it, is to tell myself that if I get through the work that I need to, I will give myself a little reward. For instance, I may tell myself if I to get up and go to the club I can take five to 10 minutes off my treadmill exercise, which will shorten my workout routine, and I'll allow myself to sit in the hot tub for a few extra minutes. Hey, it works!

Other examples: Maybe you are a mortgage broker who feels like sleeping in. Tell yourself that after the next three mortgages you close you will take your kids to the fair, or your spouse to the movies. Maybe you'll give yourself a night on the town with old friends.

Reconnect the action with pleasure rather than pain. Psychologists have long told us that we humans tend to connect every action with either pleasure or pain. Tony Robbins has popularized this even further in the last few years with something he calls Neural Associations. That is, we connect every action with either a pleasure, or pain. When we are finding ourselves lacking motivation, what we are probably finding about ourselves is that we are associating that action with pain, rather than pleasure.

For instance, when I'm considering not going to the health club on any given day, I am usually associating going and working out with having no time, the pain of exercising and weight lifting, or the boredom of running on a treadmill for an extended period of time. What I can do to re-associate is to remind myself that by going in and doing my exercise I will feel better about myself, I will lose weight, and I will live longer. This brings me pleasure. When we begin to run those kinds of tapes through our minds, we find our internal motivating force unleashed and our attitude changed about the action that we are considering.

Other examples: Maybe you are a counselor who really doesn't want to spend the day listening to people. Your association may be that it will be boring, or that you will be inside while it is sunny outside. Instead, re-associate yourself to the truth of the matter: Someone will be better off because of your care and concern. Think of your clients and the progress they have been making recently and how you have been a part of that.

Live the Life
Principle Number Six:
IT REALLY IS BETTER TO GIVE
THAN TO RECIEVE

True Success is Generous

"Write checks on a regular basis to those who you want to bless, not those who you owe. Be generous. If you are thinking of one amount, raise it a bit. They'll be glad now. You'll be glad now and later."

-- Chris Widener

There are two kinds of people in this world--those who allow their abundance to pile up and bring them a false sense of security, and those who use their abundance to increase not only the joy in their lives but also in the lives of others by being generous.

I believe that the truly successful, those who will change the lives of others and leave a legacy, are the ones who are generous with their abundance. So how do we become generous people? Here are some thoughts.

First, get over your idea that money will bring you security. It won't. It might make you feel more secure, and it might enable you to purchase things right now, but all money can disappear quite easily. Markets go south, businesses go bankrupt, and fortunes are lost. History is filled with poor people who were once rich and lost it all. This idea that we can and have to keep it all is one of the greatest myths around. So when we give money away, it doesn't affect us emotionally; it won't bring out a fear of lost security.

Second, focus on the joy you bring to others when you are generous. I love to be the one to buy something for someone who would enjoy it, to help someone who needs it, or to encourage someone who would be helped by my generosity. There are always people and organizations who will benefit from our generosity and who will be overjoyed by it. And in turn, they will help others.

> *To generous souls every task is noble.*
>
> *Euripides*

Third, make giving a planned and methodical task. I write out checks at the beginning of every month to people and organizations that I believe are helping others. I don't owe them this money, I choose to give it to them. It is something I believe in. Every month without fail I write those checks. It keeps me on track and keeps them encouraged, motivated, and moving in the right direction.

As for methodical, remember that over time, even small gifts add up. Maybe you can't afford to give or help with $300 today, but you could give $25 per month for a year. There is no way that my wife and I could afford to give a million dollars away at this stage of our lives, but our goal is to do that before we die. And I believe we will hit that because we are pursuing it methodically every month. And when we get to the end of our lives, we will be able to look back at our generosity and see that we made a difference, but you can't achieve those kinds of goals if you don't start somewhere and stick to a plan.

Fourth, make your generosity spontaneous. Now this takes a lot of self-awareness. I am not suggesting that you get yourself in financial trouble by being foolish, but:

be the generous one of the group. Pick up the check occasionally for your friends and others. I have found that if you are wise with your money you won't get yourself into trouble by being the generous one. Picking up lunch won't break the bank. Offer to do nice things for your friends, relatives and co-workers, and then watch your relationships blossom!

Fifth, understand the principle that you reap what you sow. I truly believe that those who are generous, who help others, will always receive back what they need. I live by the principle of John Wesley, "Earn all you can, give all you can, save all you can." This principle brings our finances into perfect tension. Yes we earn all that we can, but we also save and give with the same kind of gusto! Then what happens, is that we are more likely to be generous again.

> *You have to sow before you can reap. You have to give before you can get.*
>
> *Robert Collier*

Lastly, and this is key for successful people. Never allow strings with your generosity. Do not expect anything in return. That is not generosity, but manipulation. Pure generosity is its own reward.

How do you start today?

If you aren't currently on a plan of giving, choose a charitable organization you believe in and write them a check – today. Then write that same check on the first of every month.

If you are currently being generous with your resources, seriously consider an increase! Even a percentage or two will help you and them. It will stretch you and encourage them!

Be a Success! Be Generous!

Seven Things You Must Give to Others if You Want to Achieve Success!

A major part of the process of achieving success and living the kind of life that you dream of is to give. Many people think that to get what you want you have to take it. There is a universal truth though that the true path to get what you want is to give. When you give, you get. What you sow, you shall reap. If this is true, then what is it we must give? I'll show you the way...

Give Others Your Honesty. The world we live in has a simple rule that most follow: Lie when you have to. Unfortunately, this may make some people wealthy, but it makes us humans poor. To achieve success is to become wealthy not only in money, but in character. To be successful, truly successful, is to be able to attain your goals and keep your character at the same time!

"Honesty is the single most important factor having a direct bearing on the final success of an individual, corporation, or product." **Ed McMahon**

Mr. McMahon is right, though others will tell you otherwise. Some people will say, "You have to bend the truth to get ahead." Not true. Some of the most successful people who have ever lived were honest people.

How about you? Are you honest in all things? The problem with little lies is they become big ones. Lies spin out of control. You get caught in one lie and you lie to get out of it, etc.

In all things and at all times, give others your honesty.

Give Others Your Respect. Most of the time we give people respect based on what they have done or what they have accomplished. We gauge whether or not they are "worthy" of it based on what we know of what they have achieved or who they know or are related to.

I believe we should have a higher standard: We should respect people not for what they have done or for who they are related to or for what they can do for us. Instead, we should respect people for simply being.

What would happen in our world, in our company, and yes, even in our families if we started with respect for everyone else rather than making them earn it? I think we would see that most people would live up to the respect that we give them!

Give Others Your Vulnerability. We are taught to "be strong." And yes, we should be strong. But we have also embraced something that I think keeps us from having the kind of life that we long for. It is an idea that keeps us from experiencing the kind of relationships that would bring deep meaning to us. It is the idea of vulnerability.

"But Chris, make yourself vulnerable and people will step all over you!" It is true this can happen. But I have also seen that most people will be drawn to you. They will help you. They will open up to you. You see, we are all broken people inside. We all have secrets. Yet everyone plays the poser. When one lets down their veil, others soon follow – and we all win.

Give Others Your Care. Too many people are running around this old earth not caring about others. The days of "Look Out for Number One" and "Winning Through Intimidation" are over! Let's bring about a new day when we can care about others AND succeed!

Take the time to show people you care. Listen to them. Empathize with them. Love them. Now, I don't mean that you have to go around hugging everyone – that probably wouldn't fly in corporate America anyway – but we can take some time to step back from business and be human! I have found that when we do so, our business succeeds as well!

Give Others Your Passion. There is nothing this world needs more than passionate people, and people need passionate people. Living in this day and age can be tiring. The hustle and bustle of it all can wear you down and tire you out. Give your passion to others and fire them up.

Don't be humdrum – be excited. Give people all the energy you can muster up. And you will find that energy reciprocal. They will get energized and passionate. This in turn will fire you up more when you are already charged and get you going altogether when you don't feel like moving at all!

Give Others Your Experience. We all have areas in which we excel, and they are usually areas in which we have experience. One of the things we can do to make our lives more meaningful and be of utmost help to others is

Experience is not what happens to a man; it is what a man does with what happens to him.

Aldus Huxley

to show them the way through the experiences we have.

Sometimes it will be what they should do: Shortcuts to take, people to meet, etc. Sometimes it will be what they should not do: Shortcuts not to take and people to stay away from! Whatever it is, we can be of service to others by giving them our experience and ultimately, it will make us all better!

Give Others Your Help. All in all, what we want to do is to help others. Zig Ziglar says that if we will "help others get what they want, we will in turn get what we want." If we want to be successful, we should consider ourselves servants of other people. What can we do to help them and make them better? This is the true path to greatness and success, not only in business but also in life!

If you want to live the life you have always dreamed of, ask yourself if you:

- Give Others Your Honesty.
- Give Others Your Respect.
- Give Others Your Vulnerability.
- Give Others Your Care.
- Give Others Your Passion.
- Give Others Your Experience.
- Give Others Your Help.

The Art of Giving

In the pursuit of the life we dream of, this journey we are on for successful living, the focus is usually on figuring out exactly what we want and then setting ourselves on course for going to get it. This is very important: Know what you want to get for your life and then pursue it.

However, there is another aspect of achieving the life you dream of that seems on the surface to actually be counter-productive to getting the life you want, yet is imperative to the successful life. It is giving.

Giving – of yourself, your time, your money, and your energy – is something that takes us from simply being successful people in the traditional sense of the term, to being people who lead successful lives.

Giving is what makes us fully human. It is the essence of what we are, people who are here on earth together, not simply people who hope to clamber to the top of the pile in the survival of the fittest. Yes, pursue your life and your success with wild abandon; be responsible for yourself and take ownership of your life, realizing that you cannot be responsible for others, but also allow yourself to become a giving person.

Giving is also what allows us to accomplish things far beyond ourselves; and that is part of what living the life of our dreams is all about, right? Accomplishing great things through ourselves – and others!

How do we do that? Here are some ideas:

Make your giving purposeful. Give to people and organizations that fulfill purposes that you believe in. This way, they feel good, you feel good, and the work you believe in gets done. Giving purposefully will give you the ability to know that your giving is doing something great.

> *The more credit you give away, the more will come back to you. The more you help others, the more they will want to help you.*
>
> *Brian Tracy*

Make your giving proactive. Take control of your giving. When we control our giving it becomes proactive rather than reactive. We know that we are doing what we want to do rather than what others may manipulate us to do, and we can avoid a lot of the wondering about validity that comes when we give out of reaction. Giving proactively will give you peace of mind.

Make your giving generous. Don't be a tightwad! Loosen up the purse strings a bit. Think of your giving in regard to how you can be generous, not how you can cover your charitable bases. I have found that it isn't the extra money given to charity that breaks people. It is usually mismanagement. And at the end of your life, you may not know the difference financially, though you will in your heart. Making your giving generous allows you to give even greater amounts over time.

Make your giving increase. Don't just give the same amount from year to year – increase your giving. I think there are two appropriate times to adjust your giving: The first of the year and any time your income goes up. Bump your giving up then, if you can. This will keep you on pace with your giving goals and you will notice the increase less from your bottom line. Make your giving increase and your giving will keep pace with your income.

Make your giving from the heart. Don't just let your giving be a mind issue. Let it be a heart issue. This is what gives us our humanity. What causes your eyes to tear up? What causes really mean something to your heart when you are honest with yourself? Start giving to these causes! Let your checkbook be a reflection of your heart! Make your giving from the heart and you will allow your heart to grow.

(Sometimes) Make your giving spontaneous. Sometimes... Allow yourself to be spontaneous with your giving. Do allow yourself to react sometimes. Will you get taken advantage of? Yes, sometimes, but you will also be doing something within yourself that will keep you from becoming cynical. Sometimes, as life has been good to you and you find yourself blessed, let yourself be a blessing to someone else. Make your giving spontaneous (sometimes) and you will battle the disease of cynicism about charity that can creep in.

These are just a few ideas that you can implement right now to begin the art of giving in your life. The key is to decide that you will become a giver, and not merely a taker. You will choose to leave something behind in this world and not merely try to get something out of it. As we all commit to that, our world will be a better place and we can all live the lives we dream of.

Live the Life
Principle Number Seven:
RELATIONSHIPS ARE THE
CORE OF OUR EXISTENCE

The Power in Praising People

One of the keys to success is to have successful relationships. We are not islands, and we don't get to the top by ourselves. One of the key ways to grow successful in our relationships is to be "life-giving" people to others. With every person we meet, we either give life to or take life from. You know what I mean. There are people who encourage you and when your time is done with them you feel built up. Then there are others who you feel torn down by. Successful people are people who have mastered the art of building others up.

> *There are two things people want more than sex and money... recognition and praise.*
>
> *Mary Kay Ash*

One of the ways we build people up is to praise them. There is power in praising people! Something begins to happen in them, in you, and in your relationship when you praise someone. Remember a time when someone told you something about yourself in a praising manner? It was great, wasn't it? You probably liked that person more after they praised you, didn't you?

83

Now I am not talking about praising people for the sake of praising people. I am talking about honestly looking for and praising positive character traits and action of others around you. Don't lie to people. If they have done something wrong, correct it, but when they do something right, Praise it!

With that said, here are benefits of and ways to start praising people.

Benefits

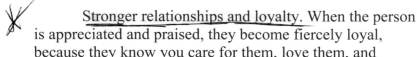

Your relationship grows. Life is about relationships. Family relationships, friends, and co-workers. When we begin to praise people for their positive aspects, our relationships grow. It puts them, and us, on the fast track.

> *I have yet to find the man, however exalted his station, who did not do better work and put forth greater effort under a spirit of approval than under a spirit of criticism.*
>
> *Charles M. Schwab*

Your leadership and influence grows. Who is going to have greater leadership and influence capacity in the lives of their followers, the one who tears down or the one who builds up?

Stronger relationships and loyalty. When the person is appreciated and praised, they become fiercely loyal, because they know you care for them, love them, and appreciate them. This will take you to success.

Happier, more fulfilled people. I truly believe it is our job to build others up and that they need it. It is a good thing in and of itself to invest in the lives of others by praising and encouraging them. Even if we never get anything in return, it is the right thing to do to build up other people. Someone else will always come along to tear them down; the successful person will instill in them the power of praise!

Some ways to praise

Character traits. Is there someone you know who is joyful? Hard-working? Honest? Then let them know how much you appreciate that in them. You can do it with a word or a card, or a phone call. Say something like this, "You know Tom, I think it is great that you are such a hard-worker. It seems like you are always the first one here and the last one to leave. You really set a good example, and I want you to know how much I appreciate that." Simple!

Action. Same idea as above. "Sue, I don't know if anybody else has told you this, but your work on the Johnson account was excellent. You have a wonderful ability to communicate the vision of the project and that helps all of the rest of us with our roles and tasks. Thanks for that. It is greatly appreciated."

Other ways you can show praise and appreciation is with a card, a gift, or time off from work.

Make it your goal to praise at least five people a day. If you can, praise ten people a day. Or perhaps you can try to praise everyone you come in contact with. It will take work, but it is possible. It just takes discipline and a little work. Any way you cut it though, there is power in praising people. First for them, then for you!

Success Through a Supercharged Network

I have finally come to believe something about myself because so many people have said the same thing to me – I mean the EXACT same sentence – over the past year. It is about something about me that others notice, which quite frankly, just comes so naturally to me that I never noticed before. It is a characteristic that, when applied to your life, will enable you to live the life you have always dreamed of because it will put you in the middle of relationships that will literally propel you to success! You see, no one lives their dreams without a lot of help from other people. I know a lot of successful people and all along the way, they all had others who went to bat for them and gave them a helping hand.

So, you are probably wondering what it is that I discovered about myself, aren't you?

Here is what I hear a lot:

"Chris, you know more people than anyone I know."

Here are some other variations:

"Chris, you are the most connected person I know."

"Chris, your network includes almost everyone!"

So I started thinking about it and I realized some things.

In the last year I have put people together, as in "Call this guy. He'll help you. Tell him I told you to call," so many times that I am guessing there will be at least $500,000 worth of business done and maybe that much again in salaries made.

Do you remember the "Six Degrees of Separation" principle? It says that most people on earth are connected by only six people connections – i.e. I know you know Joe who knows Sue, etc., until you get to the other person. Most people can do this with any other person in just six degrees. The more connected you are, the less degrees – and the easier it is to accomplish what you want to accomplish. So I started thinking and I came to the conclusion that most connections for me are two degrees and even the "toughies" are just three. Don't ask me to pass word on to the President though – he's busy!

Now, let me say this: I am not bragging at all (though I am sure it sounds like it, which is why I was a little reluctant to write about this topic). In reality, this is something I had never really thought about until just recently.

After thinking about it, I believe ANYONE – yes, even you - can have the same kinds of network! ANYONE! Why do I believe this? Because I started thinking about what has made my network so supercharged, and it comes down to a few simple basics that anyone can do. I am no better than anyone else. My Supercharged Network has nothing to do whatsoever with me being any more talented or intelligent than anyone else! It has to do with a basic understanding of human nature and the nature of relationships as well as how to apply some principles that will maximize your relationships so you can live the life you have always dreamed of!

You can have a Supercharged Network too! Here are ten "secrets" to success through a supercharged network.

1. Be successful. Successful people are sought out. If you succeed at what you put your mind and heart to, you will be sought out by other successful people. Yes, many unsuccessful people will seek you out as well, but that is the high price you pay to put yourself into the rank of those who succeed! Do your best, accomplish much and watch your network grow!

2. Be nice. If you are a jerk, people will write you off and will quit taking your phone calls, as well as avoid the people you recommend. I am amazed at how many people will sabotage their own success because they aren't nice to people.

3. Love to learn. Developing a network is about learning. You need to learn about each person you come in contact with. You need to learn human nature. You need to learn how people work together. This is fascinating stuff! If you do this simply to network, people will realize you are a phony, and phonies get left outside of the network. I truly love to learn!

4. Like people. I genuinely like people. There is always a mystery with people, always something new and exciting. Okay, sometimes they burn you, but generally speaking I like people – and that gets noticed. People like to be liked. They like to take phone calls from people who like them. They like to do business with people who are referred by people who like them. Don't pretend to like people – like people!

5. Listen. Listen to people. Listen to what makes them tick. Listen to their likes and dislikes. Listen to their dreams and fears. Listen to their hobbies. Listen to what they do. I once got a job for a guy who I couldn't even explain what he did. But I knew enough to know that when a guy I was standing next to in an elevator (3000 miles from my home) was talking about something I didn't understand, the two things I didn't understand matched up! I turned to the guy in the elevator and told him I knew just the guy for the job he was talking about. He looked condescendingly at me as though I couldn't possibly understand what he was talking about (give him credit – I didn't), and assured me that I was probably mistaken. This was a very niche job he assured me. I simply asked him for the website address and the position. He told me the website and that the position was for the CEO job. Within an hour my friend sent an email to my "friend" in the elevator. Two weeks later he was the CEO of the company! B-I-N-G-O!

6. Pursue "big-shots." Face it; big-shots know more people than little-shots! So it helps to know big-shots. Now this takes some chutzpah! First, you have to deal with your own self-esteem. You have to understand that you are more worthy than you think you are. Secondly, you have to deal with your esteem of the big-shot. Big-shots are really just little-shots with a bigger title (And they are usually more interesting. Think about it: Even a pompous blowhard big-shot is more interesting than a pompous blowhard little-shot. One brags about how they sat around and watched reruns while the other sits around bragging how they took over another company, which is definitely more interesting).

Most of the big-shots I know are the nicest people you would want to know. Very few of them are jerks or think too highly of themselves. Once you figure this out, call them and introduce yourself. Go up to them at the meeting and say hello. Note: This doesn't mean bother them at dinner or inappropriate times – I have seen famous people in public and my friends will say, "Let's go talk to him." I NEVER do. They are busy with their families for crying out loud! Bugging them is the best thing you can do to CLOSE your network. What I would do is walk past and nonchalantly nod hello to them. They will appreciate that you knew who they were and left them alone. Then, if you need to, drop them a line or call their office. They will remember you and return the favor for not bugging them like everyone else does!

7. Be helpful. Help those who you network with. Always be helpful. If someone needs something you can provide for him or her, or someone you know can provide for them, be sure to offer the help. Nothing bonds a friendship (and that is really what we are talking about here – I want as many friends as I can get) like helping someone out. I can't tell you how many times someone has been saying that they needed this or that and I said, "Do you know so and so? He can help you." They got the phone number and usually a few weeks later they call to say thanks. Additionally, this only builds on itself as your network grows.

Help others via those who you network with. Here is what I mean. Give people the opportunity to help other people. For example, one time I knew someone who was going on a medical mission and needed to get some pharmaceutical supplies soon and at cost. I knew virtually no one in the industry, but I did know an executive of a large company in a state that has more than its share of drug companies. I figured he had to know somebody. It was a shot in the dark, but it worked and the executive felt great being able to tap his network for the sake of needy kids in another country.

8. Keep records. Names, dates, phone numbers, addresses--anything to help you remember people. Harvey Mackay has his "Mackay 66" which I think is too long, but it is the right idea. Take notes and use the information to build your network. Somebody needs tickets to a State U. football game? Call that lady in accounting that graduated there. She can help!

9. Give more than you ask for. Ultimately you have to be more of a giver than a taker. Otherwise, you are more of a leech on the side of a network than you are a part of the network. Give to others any time you can help, have the resources, or know someone who does. This will make you a valuable asset in the network and people will want you around and active in the network.

10. Be social. The final idea is simply to be social. The more people you know, the wider your network will be. Not everyone will be a big part of your working network, but even those who aren't offer you one of the most cherished things on earth – friendship.

If you want to be successful in this life it will take the help of other people. We pursue relationships for relationships sake, not to use people. But we are wise enough to know that the people we develop friendships with are people who we can help and be helped by – so all of us can achieve our dreams! Take the above to heart and you will surely Supercharge Your Network – which in turn will put you on track to live the life of your dreams!

How to Talk to Anybody, Anytime

You know the situation: There you are at a business or social function and you end up with someone who you have never met before. Some people get amazingly uncomfortable with this situation because they simply don't know how to start or carry on a conversation. Yet successful people will always find themselves in these kinds of situations because they are always stretching themselves and putting themselves into situations to help them and their businesses grow, and that means meeting new people. So if you are going to be successful, one thing you have to get good at is how to talk to anybody, anytime. Good news: It is easier than you think!

First, a couple of things not to do. One, don't get flustered and excuse yourself. That is the easy way out, and you never know if you didn't just leave who would have become your best friend or closest business associate. Stick around! Secondly, don't start talking about yourself. Sure, introduce yourself, but don't launch into a half-hour monologue about your accomplishments. The other person will either roll their eyes back into their head or simply give you a new nickname: Joe "let me tell you a story about myself" Schmoe. This leads me to the key.

Talk about the person you have just met. Don't talk about yourself – talk about them! And the key is to ask questions. Now, there are obviously some people you just will not be able to talk to because they are angry or upset or something, but I have found that that is only about 1% of the people, if even that. For the most part, if you persist in asking questions, you will be able to talk to anybody, anytime.

There are three segments to this process:

- Ask questions.
- Find connections.
- Go in those directions.

What you are trying to do is to find common ground. What makes people afraid to talk to others is that they are afraid they won't have anything in common. I have found that usually, if you ask questions for a minute or two, you can always find a connection with someone, and then you're set. The worst that could happen is

> *A prudent question is one-half of wisdom.*
>
> *Francis Bacon*

that you ask the person questions for a few minutes and find nothing. But what will that person tell others? That you seem to have a genuine interest in others. That is a great reputation to have!

That is another key here. You can't be a selfish, arrogant person and be successful. I am talking true well-rounded success, not just collecting a pot full of money.

The best way to describe this process is to write out a mock conversation. You will notice below the kinds of questions I ask, and when I find a connection, how I would go in that direction.

"Hi, I'm Chris Widener. What is your name?"

"Joe Schmoe."

"Well, Joe, what do you do for a living?"

"I sell insurance." (Possible connection here. Everybody has insurance.)

"Oh yeah? What kind of insurance?"

"I insure oil rigs in the Adriatic Sea." (Whoops. Lost connection)

"Wow. That's must be fascinating. Married or kids, Joe?" (I have a wife and kids, maybe we can show pictures.)

"No, actually, I'm single." (It isn't looking good yet.)

"So, who do you know here at the party?"

"Well, nobody. I am the brother of the host's accountant. I'm in town for a week and my brother had to make an appearance." (It is going in the wrong direction here.)

"So where are you from?"

"Nebraska." (Bingo, there it is--the connection! Now let's go in that direction.)

"Really? My dad was from Nebraska. Even though he died when I was four, my grandmother used to take me back to visit my relatives every summer growing up. It sure was a lot of fun. Were you city folk, or did you live on a farm?"

"I grew up on a pig farm."

"That's what my relatives did! As a kid I always wanted to ride one of those sows. Luckily my uncles never let me attempt it."

There you are. Now just start asking questions about what they did growing up, how they liked it, etc.

If you get adept enough at asking questions of others, you will inevitably find a connection to talk about. And having something in common with someone is the start to a long and mutually beneficial relationship – one of the foundations of success!

I am in a career where I meet new people all the time, and this is exactly what I do. I am no better conversationalist than you. It is just a proven way of getting a relationship off the ground with someone you have just met.

Here it is again:

Ask questions, find connections, go in those directions.

Live the Life
Principle Number Eight:
DON'T TIP – KEEPING YOUR BALANCE

The Myth of What We Manage

Perhaps it is merely semantics, but an underlying problem I find that people have as it relates to the success in their life lies in a proper understanding of what exactly it is that we manage. Think about it. We have time management (In fact I have a seminar on this very topic, some of which is excerpted below), and financial management, and relational management, weight management, career management, and many, many more.

The fact is though, that we don't manage any of those things. What we do manage is ourselves, as they relate to those things. We don't manage time. Time clicks by, second by second, whether we do anything or not. What we do is manage ourselves, and our activities, as the time passes. We make choices as to what we will do and be involved in. The problem as well as the solution, lies not with time, but with us.

We don't manage money. A pile of money will sit there forever if left alone. It won't grow or shrink. What we manage is ourselves and the decisions we make in regard to how we will spend the money. Getting the idea?

So as we live our lives and pursue success, one of the keys to grab onto is the idea that the most important thing we can manage isn't a thing at all – it is our self!

How then can we manage ourselves? Here are some thoughts.

Make sure that the above is firmly engrained in your thinking: I only manage myself. I can choose how I will act and react in every situation. Dwight D. Eisenhower said, "The history of free men is not written by chance, but by choice, their choice."

Know your priorities. Do you know from top to bottom what your priorities are? Have you decided on the top ten things where you want to spend your time? How about the same with your money? Only after you know these things can you properly manage yourself into choosing to live your priorities.

Learn to say "no" with a smile on your face. Here is where most of us fail. We do not choose to say "no" to those things that are not a matter of priority (the reason "why" is another newsletter article and probably a few counseling sessions at that!). Someone calls us up and asks us to do something for them (usually because they haven't managed themselves and would like our help picking up the pieces) and we say "Uh, I guess so." Then what? We usually kick ourselves for the rest of the day. "Why did I ever say yes?" Instead, practice this, "Gee, I am really sorry, but I am not going to be able to be involved this time. I am sure you will be able to find somebody though." Go ahead and try it right now. Weird, isn't it? That is because we don't say it very often.

Schedule your priorities into your schedule or budget or whatever structure governs that area of your life. For example, do you have a financial budget that you yourself set? Then do you first and foremost spend your money in that way, say at the beginning of the month? If you do, you will eliminate even the opportunity to blow your money on impulse decisions and expenses because your money has already been committed to your priorities.

Remember, one of the greatest gifts God gave us is the ability to choose. And we can choose to manage ourselves appropriately and according to our priorities. As we do, we will find ourselves feeling less and less of the personal pain and frustration that we feel when we are out of control.

Get goin'!

Bringing Balance to a Chaotic Life

If I had to make a composite question that gets at the heart of the question that I am asked most frequently, it would be this: How can I manage my time more effectively and bring balance to my life in regard to work, family, friends, and social obligations?

With this in mind, I want to give some thoughts to focus on for the answer to that question.

I am convinced that the most important thing we must do is to be acutely aware of the reasons we should manage our time and bring balance to our lives. In fact, most of us really know "how" to do it, don't we? Then why don't we? I think it comes to the issue of having a powerful motivating factor or reason. Below are two of mine that keep me motivated:

A life of accomplishment. When I am old and unable to get out with the young folks anymore, I want to be able to look back on my life and say that I accomplished much and that my life benefited others. That is why I do what I do now. It is what drives me to pursue what I pursue with a passion and vigor. It is why I bring my life into balance in many areas--so I can achieve much in many areas.

A legacy. Here is a powerful motivating image that I picture with regularity: Picture a family gathering five years after your death. What will it look like? What will the people be talking about? How will they remember you? What will be the quality of their lives and how will you have been instrumental in that? These are questions that we can for the most part, answer now by how we live our lives (for better or for worse). Our lives make a difference in the lives of others! This is a tremendous reason to bring my life into balance!

Once we answer the "Why" question, and root it firmly in our minds and hearts, we come to the "how's."

First, we sit down and prioritize. Have you ever taken a couple of hours and listed everything that you are involved in or could be involved in and then prioritized it by importance? You may come up with a hundred items, but that is okay. You will want to separate them into categories as well, such as Work, Family, Health, Friends, Hobbies, Spiritual, Financial, Intellectual, Emotional, etc.

Now you have something to look at and see what is important. This will help you in the process of eliminating areas from your life where you are spending time that you shouldn't be, and that is an important part: Frustration comes when we get involved in something that isn't a priority and we kick ourselves the whole time we do it. If we stick to priorities, we eliminate much of that.

The next step is to learn the most powerful word in the human language: No. Just look in the mirror and practice saying that word with a smile on your face. This may be the most important part – learning to decline opportunity. It all depends on whether or not it fits in with our priorities.

Here is the principle that drives this:

Good is the enemy of the best.

There are lots of good things we can spend our time on, but because they replace those things that would be the best things we could spend our time on, they become our enemy. They become counter-productive to a successful and balanced life.

So ask yourself: Is this good? Or is it the best? Do the best you can to stick to the best!

Schedule your time. The more we fly by the seat of our pants, the more apt we are to lose control of our time. If we schedule out our time, we can become a bit more objective and bring our lives into balance. For example, you may make it your goal to be home by six o'clock every night. In your schedule book, you write in that you have an appointment at six. You schedule to leave the office at five-thirty. Now when a co-worker comes in with an "opportunity" for you to work on, you say, "Sorry, I have an appointment at six that I can't break. Let's get together on it first thing in the morning." Scheduling your time, coupled with saying "no," will do wonders for bringing your life into balance!

Another aspect for us to look at is the area of external pressure that causes us to be out of balance. For example, financial obligations may be what keep us working too much. So we should look at those obligations and see if we can eliminate or reduce them.

The last thing I would challenge you with is to give some thought as to what the secret pleasures of being out of balance may be. For example, sometimes we let ourselves over commit because we don't like conflict. Peace is our secret pleasure.

Sometimes we allow ourselves to become out of balance because we like it when people say, "Boy, she sure is a dynamo. Look how busy she is." Admiration from others is our secret pleasure.

In review:

- Find the right reasons
- Set priorities
- Learn to say "no"
- Understand that the good is the enemy of the best
- Schedule your time
- Manage External pressures
- Be aware of internal "secret pleasures"

A Little Equation that Creates Big Results

Often people will ask me how I get so much done in my life. They wonder at how I am able to accomplish so many things. The answer is found not in what a great person I am, but in an equation I came up with a few years ago and remind myself of almost on a daily basis. When I live this equation out, it produces big results. What people don't seem to grasp is that this equation will work for anybody! Anyone can see results in their life if they will live it out!

This little equation, when it is understood, and acted upon, is perhaps the most powerful equation there is in regard to long-term achievement and accomplishment. Yet, it is not complex. In fact, it is rather simple. So what is it?

Your short-term actions multiplied by time equals your long-term accomplishments.

If you want to see change in your life, see big results, the first thing you must do is change your current actions. Otherwise, the old saying becomes a reality: "If you always do what you've always done, you'll always get what you always got!" But if we change our actions, we will see different results!

Most people want to accomplish a lot in their lives, yet very few actually do. Why is this? It is because what they believe produces their long-term accomplishments is wrong. Here are some of the things people believe will create great accomplishments for them:

- Beliefs
- Vision
- Big dreams

- Ideas
- Ideals
- Values
- Desire

The truth is that while these things are very important, they are not enough in and of themselves. We need to have the above underlying all that we do, but we need to actually do something! And this is where most people stop. We need to take action on our dreams and beliefs every day.

Here are some examples of how this works.

Who loses weight? The one who knows all about the benefits of exercise or the one who walks 3 miles a day?

Who retires early? The one who dreams of a house on the beach, or the one who invests $300 a month?

Who writes books? The one who desires to become a best-selling author, or the one who gets up early and writes for half an hour a day?

Who has the best marital relationship? The one who knows how much spending time with their spouse can improve their relationship, or the one who sits down and talks with their spouse every night?

> *The purpose of man is in action, not thought.*
>
> *Thomas Carlyle*

Who makes the most sales? The one who believes they can become a great salesperson, or the one who makes 10 sales calls a day?

I think you get the point. When it all comes down to it, we must act upon our vision, beliefs, and ideals or we won't see them come to fruition. I see too many people who know what is right, but don't ever do anything about it. Imagine what a difference we could make in our own lives and the lives of others if we would simply begin to act upon on our beliefs!

When I get to the end of my life, I want to know that I have done all that I can to make this world a better place and to enhance the lives of those around me. I want to know that I gave it my best shot, and I am sure that you do, too.

I remember reading an interview with an author who has written numerous books that have sold in the tens of millions. They asked him how he did it. His answer was that he got up every morning before anyone else in his family and wrote, long hand, with a pencil, for an hour. Then he quit and went about his day. His short-term actions piled up. Seven hours a week. Thirty hours a month. Three hundred and sixty-five hours a year. After a while, he had lots of books!

Some questions as we leave:

What long-term accomplishments do you want to see come to pass?

What short-term actions will you need to do over time to see them come to pass?

What will you do today to begin seeing your dreams come true?

What will you do this week to see them come true?

You can have an awesome future, filled with great achievements and results if you begin today to take action and make it a reality!

One more time, so you can plug it in, memorize it, and live it.

Your short-term actions multiplied by time equals your long-term accomplishments.

Live the Life
Principle Number Nine:
ACHIEVE FINANCIAL
FREEDOM

Finding Financial Freedom

Have you ever gotten an email or letter that says something like this: "Find Financial Freedom! Make $150,000 from home in the next 90 days!"

Every time I get one of these, I think to myself, "Hmmm, Financial Freedom. I already have financial freedom, even though it doesn't look like what these emails promise me."

Financial freedom is a buzzword for our generation. It is the pursuit of literally millions of people. So what is it? Is it that elusive? Can anyone get it?

Let me start by saying that this chapter will not be about how to earn money, or even more money. Rather, it will be about how to find financial freedom, which may or may not involve making more money.

Financial freedom – here we go!

The first step in finding financial freedom is to realize that financial freedom has absolutely nothing to do with how much money you have or make. What? Exactly. Financial freedom is something that goes on inside of you. This is why someone who makes very little can be happy and someone who makes a ton can be extremely stressed out over his or her financial situation. So the first step is to realize that financial freedom is more about our attitudes toward money than about the amount of money.

"Okay Chris, I'm with you. So what are the attitudes that provide financial freedom?" Here are a few that keep me in financial freedom.

I do not have to worry about money. I used to catch myself saying, "If I had more money, then I wouldn't have to worry about …" But do you know what? I don't have to worry anyway. I can control my income. I can control my outgo. I can make choices that can alleviate any of my worries. I also realized that things always work out. So why worry? I choose not to worry.

> *Each man makes his own prison.*
>
> *Sir Edwin Arnold*

I can be happy regardless of my financial state. I know people who are worth hundreds of millions of dollars, and I know people who don't have two nickels to rub together. Some are happy and some aren't. And none of the people who have a lot of money say to me, "Chris, I've become so happy since I got money." They were happy before they had money and they are happy now that they have money. Their happiness has nothing to do with the money. I think it was the Billionaire David Geffen who said, "Anyone who says that money will buy them happiness has never had any money."

Money will be a means to an end, not the end itself. Another way to look at it is that money will be a tool to build the house, not the house itself. I would set some financial goals if I were you, but go beyond that to know what greater purpose there will be when you reach them. What will the house be that you will build with that tool?

I am free. I am free to earn – some people think it is bad to earn more money. It isn't. I am free to save – some people believe it is bad to save. It isn't. I am free to give money away – some people feel they will be better off hoarding

> *No man is free who is not a master of himself.*
>
> *Epictetus*

it. They won't. I am free to spend – some people believe that they can't spend anything on themselves. They can. We are free to make choices. That is financial freedom. One of my favorite quotes is from Charles Wesley, "Earn all you can, save all you can, give all you can." That will keep you in financial freedom.

Some other principles for financial freedom...

Debt is the primary freedom killer. Want financial freedom? The first thing you should do is to get out of debt. That is priority number one. One of the reasons I have financial freedom is that I have no debt other than my house payment, and I work hard to manage myself and our home to keep us that way. For years I drove an old junker car, and while it looked bad, I had financial freedom that others who were in debt didn't have!

There is an old proverb – The borrower is the servant of the lender. Who has freedom? The lender. Who doesn't? The borrower. Develop a plan to get out of debt!

Embrace delayed gratification. Here is the principle: Buy it now and struggle later. Another principle: Delay it now, invest the money, and have all you want later on! And you won't even have to touch the principal! We tend to think that having it now will bring enjoyment, but unless you can do it and not cause yourself financial stress, you will actually get more from waiting to buy it later!

Have more by managing better. The fact is that most of us earn enough. What would be beneficial is to set our priorities and live by a budget. As we get control, our budget will loosen up a bit and we will find ourselves enjoying it more. Money that is already there can be your answer if you put it to work for you.

Spend some time thinking through your attitudes about money. You may be surprised at how you can change a few of your attitudes, look at things a little bit differently and begin to enjoy true financial freedom!

The Financial Equation that Will Set You Free!

I have a good friend who works in an area of the US that has more than its share of poverty. He called me the other day with a very broken heart. He was feeling badly for the people around him who simply do not allow themselves to get set free financially. I could feel the pain he was feeling because I too, very often wonder why it is that some people experience financial independence and others do not. It really is a mystery.

But how to get financial independence is not a mystery!

Rather, financial independence is a very simple thing. Truly! It is hard work and takes time, but the process is very simple! In fact, financial independence can come from following a very simple plan. All of the books on financial independence can ultimately be boiled down to this basic equation. It is an equation that is as simple as it gets. In fact, it isn't even a multiplication problem, it is an addition equation! And we all learned addition in the first grade! Just as $1 + 1 = 2$, so does this POWERFUL yet SIMPLE equation add up to your financial independence!

What is this equation? Get ready, your life is about to change forever if you will allow yourself to understand and live by the simplicity of this equation. Here it is:

Smart Decisions + Good Math = Financial Independence

Let's break it down and take a closer look. First the Smart Decisions, then the Good Math.

Smart Decisions:

Go to college. Get educated. I know that somebody will say, "Yeah, but most of the people on the Forbes 400 never went past high school." Well, so did most of the people in the welfare line! Most people aren't Bill Gates or Sam Walton. Most people who earn between $100,000-$150,000 a year are college graduates. "But I'm forty! I can't go to college." Yes you can. You will be 44 when you get out and have 21 years of a much better income. The fact is that most good jobs and careers go to those who have educated themselves. It is still the surest way to a long-term large income.

Still don't want to go to college? See the last item under smart decisions.

Get better training. At the very least go get some training in your specific area of expertise. The promotions will go to those who are the best trained, so become the best trained! Take a course, even if your employer won't pay for it, because eventually they WILL pay you for it!

Work hard. I have found that the many hundreds of high achievers who I know personally who have become and are becoming financially independent are hard workers. Every one of them works long hours. They sacrifice for the security they are shooting for and have attained. I know, we all get advertisements that say, "Financial Independence in 10 hours a week." Let me ask you, do you know anybody like that? I don't. Not one. Even the success stories you hear in the get rich quick industries show you that they worked HARD!

Develop yourself. Become a better person. Better people get better jobs and get paid better dollars! Make sure that every day you are becoming a person who is on the growth track, raising yourself to a higher and higher level with each and every passing day! Eventually your development will catch up with you and your income will soar!

Stay out of debt. This is the smartest decision you will ever make. NO Debt! You know what? I have ONE bill I have to pay every month. That is my mortgage. But that's a debt, right? Well, without getting into an argument, I consider it a forced investment with the added

> *Debt is the worst poverty.*
>
> *Thomas Fuller*

benefit of providing shelter for my family and me! I do not consider a mortgage a debt. I am talking about car debt, stereo debt, and consumer debt of all kinds. It is possible. It can be done, and it will provide you with financial freedom!

Own your own business if you can. So you don't want to go to college? Okay. Or maybe you did go to college and you just want to make sure that you earn as much as you can. Well, the smart decision is to own your own business. Most millionaires in America are the people who own their own businesses. It will take a lot of risk, a lot of hard work, and many ups and downs, but owning your business gives you the opportunity to accumulate great wealth, because the profit is all yours. There are plenty of opportunities to own your own business, and I would encourage you to strongly consider the alternative for many reasons, one of the best of which is the opportunity to achieve financial independence.

Good Math:

Spend less than you earn. One plus one equals two. We learn that very early on. Eventually, we learn negatives and we learn that one minus two equals negative one. Simple right? Yet many people live their lives in such a way that they spend more than their income and destroy their opportunity for long-term financial independence. There are two things you can do to make this "good math" work for you. You can increase your income so that it outpaces your spending, or you can decrease your spending. You increase your income by making the smart decisions listed above. You decrease your spending by making hard choices. You may have to give up spending on things that you really like. One of these must be done if you are going to achieve the kind of long-term financial independence you desire.

Put money away into investment vehicles on a regular basis. If you are going to achieve financial independence, you will have to put away money regularly. This is the math principle of addition. Don't laugh: most people don't get this. Or if they do, they don't practice it! Whether it is every paycheck, or the first of the month, or quarterly, or however you can do it – DO IT! When you hit 65 years of age, you will be glad you did. And if you put away enough and into the right investments, you may just be thankful a lot sooner than that!

Let your interest accrue. This is the law of compounding interest and it is powerful! If you earn twelve percent on your money every year, do you know how soon it will be until you have twice as much as you started with? At first thought you may assume that it is one hundred divided by twelve, or eight and a third years. Not true. There is an investment rule that is called the rule of 72. That is, divide 72 by what average interest you make and that is how many years it takes to double your money. In this case, at twelve percent, your money doubles every six years! This works because you earn twelve percent on not only the original amount, but the interest you earned as well.

Start with $100 and the next year you have $112. If you take the $12 out then you will only make twelve percent on $100 again. If you let it accrue, you will make twelve percent on $112. This will cut over two years off of the time it takes to double your money!

Where the real power comes in is over longer periods of time. Let's say grandma dies and leaves you $25,000 when you are eighteen. You can do any number of things with that money.

Buy a snazzy car. Not a good idea, though most eighteen year-olds would do just this.

Invest the money and take out the interest every year. This is nice. It throws you $3000 every year and over forty-two years you make $126,000 for doing nothing and you still have $25,000! Not bad, not bad at all.

Here is the real deal! You leave the money alone for forty-two years at twelve percent (about the long-term average for the stock market). At the end of that time you decide to retire and go to the investment summary to see how much you have. What do you find? You find that your money doubled seven times and that leaves you with 3.2 million dollars! Can you retire on that? You bet you can.

You can achieve financial independence. You can live the financial life you have always dreamed of. You can have a life where you have enough at all times, especially in the end. It is possible. You just have to make smart decisions and use good math!

As a refresher, here they are again:

Smart decisions:

- Go to college.
- Get better training.
- Work hard.
- Develop yourself.
- Stay out of debt.
- Own your own business if you can.

Good math:
- Spend less than you earn.
- Put money away into investment vehicles on a regular basis.
- Let your interest accrue.

Live the Life
Principle Number Ten:
Attitude Is King

<u>Five Attitudes that Will Make You Soar!</u>

Understand this: Much of your world, and your experience in it, will be a direct result of the attitude you choose to have. Let me break that statement down a bit:

One, attitude is MUCH of your world. Yes, there are some things that just happen and there is nothing we can do about it, but much of our world is not by happenstance, but determined by the attitudes we take.

Two, your attitude is one that you choose. You do not have to have a chip on your shoulder. You do not have to be sad

> *Life is the movie you see through your own eyes. It makes little difference what's happening out there. It's how you take it that counts.*
>
> *Denis Waitley*

or angry. You do not have to believe that you are incapable of achieving success. We can choose at any moment how we will believe and how we will interact with the world.

Third, our experience is a direct result of our attitude. For example, if we have a bad attitude toward someone, what kind of attitude do you think we are going to get back? That's just the people side, but that makes up most of our world right there!

So, if our attitudes determine to a great degree what kind of life we will have, shouldn't we focus in on the best attitudes to have and then make them ours? Absolutely! If we want to soar with the eagles in this life, and if there are attitudes that will make us soar, shouldn't we pursue them with all our hearts? By all means! So here we go!

Five attitudes that will make you soar!

"I can." This is the most basic of all attitudes. We simply must choose to believe that we can. In our house we are not allowed to say, "I can't." We can say, "I'll try," or "I tried and failed," but not "I can't." Telling yourself that you can't, will in effect make it so you can't. But telling yourself that you can, will in effect enable you to achieve much more. Even if you actually only achieve 50% of what you tell yourself you can achieve, you will achieve at least that much more than if you told yourself you couldn't.
I actually have a standard way of going about getting myself off of the starting block: I simply say if somebody else has, then I can, too. And if many others have, then surely I can, too! I have to be smarter than at least one of those who has already done it. I have to be able to work harder than at least one other. There has to be at least one other person who has come from more difficult circumstances than me. And if they can do it then certainly, "I can!"

"I will be generous." Another attitude that will make you soar is to be a generous person. The attitude (and discipline) of generosity increases your likelihood of success for two main reasons: One, you are happier about yourself and that puts you in a state of mind that is prepared for successful living. Two, people pay back people who are generous. Generous people receive in kind, and that will raise you to levels yet unseen.

"I will make a difference in the lives of those around me." People who soar are generally people who have the attitude of helping other people. Yes, they may do it for monetary gain, but they are others-focused. They want to change the way people live and experience life for the better. They are difference makers all around. I live in a town that is very affluent. Most of the people I know, work with, and have as friends are very successful in this world. One thing I can say, as almost a universal truth, is that they are people who are not self-consumed but genuinely care about others and will do what they can to help others. This is what I know to be true about the attitudes of the genuinely successful.

"Not much will make me angry." Whether or not we get angry is a choice of attitude. We determine whether or not we will be angry. I have found that often I will meet with someone who is struggling with achieving something and in many cases I find that they are angry people. They have held onto an attitude that is angry at its root. When we take on an attitude that raises the bar on what will make us angry, we are positioning ourselves to be in a state of mind that is better able to live and work in this world in such a way as to achieve success.

> *To different minds, the same world is a hell, and a heaven.*
>
> *Ralph Waldo Emerson*

"I will look for the good in every situation." This is basic optimism. Successful people who soar through life are those who are optimistic about life. They see the good, think the best and strive for greatness, believing all the while that they will achieve it because it is possible!

I suppose there are a few other attitudes that would make you achieve all that you dream of, but these are the basics and ones that we would do well to master first.

Where do you see yourself? Do you need an attitude adjustment? Take a look again:

- I can.
- I will be generous.
- I will make a difference in the lives of those around me.
- Not much will make me angry.
- I will look for the good in every situation.

Make these attitudes your goal and as you get them you will watch yourself soar!

Have a nice flight!

Keeping Your Attitude Up When Circumstances Are Down

"Instead of spending your time thinking about how bad things are, think about how good they will be!"
--Chris Widener

We now know that a positive attitude is key to the successful life. But what happens when things go wrong? What happens when circumstances deal us a blow? We have a tendency to let our attitudes take the dive along with our state of affairs. Life deals us setbacks, both minor and major, on a regular basis, but if we are going to be

120

successful, we need to know how to deal with them and keep our attitudes intact! We need practical tools to help us understand how we can go about keeping our attitude up, when the circumstances are down. Here are some thoughts to help us do so:

Take some time-out. I'm sure you are aware of what happens. You are going about your day and everything seems to be going well, when out of nowhere disaster strikes. All of your best-laid plans begin to tumble. Sometimes circumstances surprise us and we react. Unfortunately, this often compounds the problem because by reacting we tend to operate out of our weaknesses instead of our strengths. We make decisions that are not well thought out. We function with a bad attitude that says, "I can't believe this is happening!"

> *How beautiful is it to do nothing, and then rest afterward.*
>
> *Unknown*

The next time circumstances turn against you, take some time to just step back from the problem and think. This will enable you to deal with the issue at hand rationally, instead of emotionally. It will allow you to put your state of mind back into its proper place. It gives you the opportunity to choose your attitude as you face the circumstances at hand. Remember that we don't have to do

> *Goals are a means to an end, not the ultimate purpose of our lives. They are simply a tool to concentrate our focus and move us in a direction.*
>
> *Anthony Robbins*

something right now. Go grab a cup of coffee and relax little bit. By doing this you function with you being in control and not the circumstances.

Keep your eye on the goal. A second step in keeping our attitude in the proper place is to make sure we keep the important things important. One of the biggest problems with trouble is that it gets your focus off of where it should be. When I experience difficult circumstances and people ask me how it is going, I tell them, "I am just keeping my eye on the goal." It has always been fascinating to me that when racecar drivers get into trouble, they keep their eyes straight ahead and do not move them away. There is just too much chance of wrecking that way. Instead, their eyes are on the goal, and this keeps them out of trouble. If you find yourself getting down about circumstances, sit down and write out what the goal is. Give some thought to how you can achieve that goal, or others you may have.

A man was asked how he was doing and he responded, "Pretty well, under the circumstances." The other man asked, "What are you doing under the circumstances?" Good question. We shouldn't be under the circumstances; we should be focused on the goal and moving forward.

Focus on solutions, not problems. The squeaky wheel gets the oil, the old saying goes. Negative circumstances don't sit idly by. They scream for our attention. When we face difficult circumstances, we tend to dwell on them. We talk about them, fret about them, and give them way too much attention. Instead of talking about problems, talk about solutions. Instead of spending your time thinking about how bad things are, think about how good they will be! Don't have family or staff meetings about the problems and how big they are. Have meetings on the solutions and how you will implement them. Don't let yourself or other team members complain. Encourage them to solve, with an emphasis on the positive results that will come from doing so. Then take some time to put these solutions down on paper, so you can monitor your progress.

Get some positive input. The mind tends to build on itself, so when we begin to go in one direction, i.e. worry, it can be a slippery slope. One thing we must do is get our thoughts back on track with positive ideas. When circumstances have got you against the emotional wall, get with a good friend who can encourage you. Listen to tapes by motivational speakers. Pick up a good book and give it a read. Whatever external influence you can get to put your attitude back on the positive side of the tracks – do it! It must be one of our first goals to start plugging good things into our minds to fuel our attitudes.

Tell yourself the good. One of the greatest internal powers we have is the power to control our thoughts. Spend time dwelling on the good things about your life or job instead of the problems. Think about positive things, things you enjoy and give you a sense of happiness and peace. There is an old childhood song that says, "Count your blessings, name them one by one." That is great advice! Let your positive attitude develop from within as well as from without. This makes all the difference!

Remember that circumstances are not forever. Sometimes it seems like we are going to be up to our eyeballs in the situation forever, when in reality, this too shall pass. There will be a time in the future when circumstances will change and you will be on the mountain instead of the valley. This will give you a sense of hope as you live and work that will change your attitude, make you feel better and put you on the fast track for growth!

Some questions:

Q. Do you have a habit of reflection before responding?

Q. Do you have a habit of keeping your eye on the goal?

Q. Do you focus on solutions or problems?

Q. Do you give yourself positive outside influence?

Q. Do you have a habit of telling yourself the good?

Q. Do you remind yourself that nothing is forever?

Are You and Optimist or a Pessimist?

"I became an optimist when I discovered that I wasn't going to win any more games by being anything else."
--Earl Weaver

I have been giving some thought lately to optimism and pessimism. Basically, these are attitudes. Attitudes that shape and formulate our entire existence. I mean, have you ever met a happy pessimist? Of course not.

In short, our optimism or pessimism is this:

- The way we interpret the past
- The way we experience and view the present
- The way we imagine the future

Have you given much thought about how your attitude, whether you are an optimist or a pessimist, affects your business, organization or school? Have you thought about how it affects you personally? And what about the team you are a part of?

What is optimism? It is a belief that things in our past were good for us, even if that means they were hard and taught us lessons. It is also the belief that things will be better in the future.

Here are some contrasts between optimism and pessimism and how they affect us:

Optimism breathes life into you each day
Pessimism drains you

Optimism helps you to take needed risks
Pessimism plays it safe and never accomplishes much

Optimism improves those around you
Pessimism drags them down

Optimism inspires people to great heights
Pessimism deflates people to new lows

There is only one way that optimism and pessimism are the same, and that is they are both self-fulfilling. If you are an optimist, you will generally find that good things happen to you. If you are a pessimist, you will find yourself in the not-so-good situations more often than not.

So can a person just become an optimist? Yes! We can choose to look at the world any way we want to. We can choose to look at the world and think the worst, or we can tell ourselves the good things about each situation. As you find yourself looking at your enterprise, begin to view it through the eyes of an optimist, and you will reap the rewards listed above, and so will the people around you.

There are tremendous benefits to being an optimist, as stated above. But there are some pessimists out there who will say, "But that isn't realistic." I say, "Who cares?" If things go awry, at least I have spent my time beforehand enjoying life and not worrying about it. And, being an optimist, I would view the "negative" situation as an opportunity to grow and learn. So I can even look forward to my failures because they will be stepping-stones, and learning tools to be applied to my future success.

Have you ever met a successful pessimist? Become an optimist and see your world change before your eyes!

<u>Your Attitude – You Choose</u>

There are lots of things in this life that we don't get to choose. On the other hand, there are lots of thing in this life that we do get to choose. Our attitude is one of the things that we get to choose. Nobody else lives inside our brain. Nobody else controls what or how we think. It is up to us, moment by moment, to choose what our attitude is. It is up to us to determine how we will look at and perceive the world around us. It is up to us to decide how we will react to our world around us.

My advice? Choose a positive, optimistic attitude! Here are some thoughts on choosing your attitude.

We cannot choose our circumstances. For the most part, this is true. We cannot control if someone around us gets ill. We cannot control how another person will treat us. We cannot control the global economy. We cannot control the direction our society as a whole will go. For some, this may seem scary. For me, it is freeing. I don't have to control my circumstances. Running the whole world would be a big responsibility. It is good to know that I am not in charge of, or in control of all of my circumstances. This dose of reality frees you to focus in on what you can control – your attitude.

We can choose our attitudes. That's right. We get to choose what our attitudes are. Here is the definition of attitude: "The feeling or opinion about something or someone, or a way of behaving that follows from this." We choose how we feel about others and situations. We choose our opinion about people and situations. We choose the way we will behave in relation to other people and circumstances.

> *Ability is what you're capable of doing. Motivation determines what you do. Attitude determines how well you do it.*
>
> *Lou Holtz*

We choose it. It doesn't have to be bad. It doesn't have to be anything but what we want it to be. We have the option.

The choice of a right attitude will significantly determine new circumstances. Choosing to have the right attitude will change the world around you. This isn't any sort of magic; it is just how the world works. Now, don't get me wrong. It won't cure everything and turn your world into a virtual Shangri-La, but it will significantly improve the world you live in. For example, let's say that every day you go into work and you gripe about life and work from the moment you get there until the moment you leave. Will others want to be around you? Will others ask your opinion? Will others like you? Will others ask you to join them for lunch? Probably not! But what if you come to work every day and you are the positive optimist of the crowd? Will everybody love you? No, but significantly more people will than if you are the office pessimist! Your choice of attitude will determine what kind of circumstances you get!

Ultimately, it is our choice on what we have as an attitude. Nobody else can force you to have a bad attitude. Nobody else can force you to have a good attitude. It is simply a choice you make.

Where are you with your attitude? Do you have a good one? Why not sit down and give it some serious thought? Then, no matter where you find yourself, decide to take your attitude to the next level! If you have a really bad attitude, decide to take it up a couple of levels!

Your attitude. Your choice. Choose wisely.

Final Words:
Lock in Your Legacy

Lock In Your Legacy

You, my friend, are going to die.

What? What kind of motivational tool is that? Real inspiring!

In fact, it is. Our mortality may perhaps be the ultimate inspiration and motivation! If we lived on this earth eternally, we could be procrastinators extraordinaire! We would never have to get anything done because there would always be tomorrow. But alas, we pass on and all we leave are the memories and the lives of others we affected while we were here. Sounds gloomy? In actuality, it is exciting! You see, this gives us purpose and a deadline. (Pun intended).

We can choose how we will live on in the hearts and memories of others. We do this by purposing to live lives NOW that make change happen in ourselves, and those around us.

What kind of legacy will you leave? How will your family and friends remember you? How will you leave your descendants in the following areas? Give some thought to them and make some changes. In doing so, you will begin to lock in your legacy.

Emotionally: Have you ever stepped back and asked yourself how you treat other people and how that effects them emotionally? I have four children, and I am acutely aware that they are being shaped emotionally by how I treat them and teach them how to deal with the world. I am especially aware of this from my own background. I can directly trace the few emotional shortcomings I have to the emotional coolness I felt from my own family. Are you raising emotionally healthy kids who are both independent as well as interdependent? Are you helping your spouse to grow emotionally? Give this some serious thought.

Spiritually: In my mind, the "God" question is the most important. You know, I often hear people say that they are just going to let their kids "figure it out on their own." These same people will show them how to shoot a basketball, trade stocks, and build a tree house, all simply temporal issues, but leave the answers to the biggest question up in the air! Now I am not advocating cramming anything down their throats, just taking the time to helping them find their way. Are you helping and encouraging those around you to find their spiritual life? Are you living an authentic spiritual life that will be your legacy? Give some serious thought to this.

Physically: Now I know what you are thinking: I can't change my genes. They got what they got and they'll have to live with it. To a certain extent this is true. I am 5'11 for the rest of my life. I will never be 6 foot, and neither will my kids. What I am talking about though, is to be examples of taking our physical health seriously. The statistics prove that whatever bad habits you have, your kids are likely to have as well. Why? Because you are their example. This is why I work to stay physically fit. I work out. I lift weights. I eat right (most of the time – I am a sucker for Breyer's Vanilla Bean Ice Cream). I don't smoke. I want to leave a legacy of health behind for my kids. True, they can still go astray, but I will do my best to give them a good example to follow. Give this some serious thought.

Financially: There are two primary ways you can leave a financial legacy. First, teach your loved ones about how to handle money (some of you may need to learn yourself first). There are just so many good books on the subject, there is no excuse for not knowing how to handle money. Rich Dad, Poor Dad is a good book to start with, or perhaps The Millionaire Next Door. These will teach you the basics. Secondly, you can leave an inheritance. Now let me be clear on this. This does not have to be after you die. In fact, the more you have, the more I believe you ought to give away while you are alive. Let's face it, the older you get, the less need you have for money once the basics are taken care of. It always cracks me up that by the time you can afford a big house, your kids are gone and you don't need one! Turn the money over early so you can watch the joy of your loved ones spending, investing and giving it! This is of course predicated upon the assumption that you have first taught them how to handle it. If you have, then you should give it away while you're alive so you can enjoy seeing your legacy in action! Give your financial inheritance some serious thought.

Relationally: What kind of legacy will you leave in regard to how people you know interact relationally with others? When people look at how you interact with others, will they be better off if they develop the same relational habits? Will your legacy be one of love, patience, kindness, faithfulness, gentleness, and forgiveness? As you live this life, you will see that your legacy grows in those you influence day by day. Give the idea of influencing others relationally some serious thought.

Intellectually: I don't know about you, but I want to challenge people to deeper intellectual thought. In a day and age of People Magazine mentalities, we need people who will challenge us to think deeper. Are you doing anything that will challenge your sphere of influence to intellectual gains? Will those left after you are gone, say that you made them think thoughts they hadn't before? That you challenged them to be smarter? Give this issue some serious thought.

Functionally: Functionally? Yep. It's a catch-all word. It is how they function. It is all of the above, rolled into one. How will those you influence actually function? This is to a great degree how you function. Are you well-rounded? Are you balanced? Do you keep the main things the main things? Is your life functioning well? Make it your goal to live a balanced, functional life so you can leave a legacy of such. Give your life function some serious thought.

I ended each paragraph with a challenge to think seriously about each. These aren't issues we will solve immediately. They take a lifetime to build and they will ebb and flow. But as you diligently pursue staying on top of them all, you will be locking in that legacy you desire to leave behind!

The fact is, you CAN live the life you have always dreamed of. It IS within your grasp if you follow the principles contained in this book.

I have worked with thousands of people from all around this world and have seen people do tremendous things when they set their hearts, minds, and hard work on their goals and dreams.

Remember, you CAN do it – and you will!

Chris Widener

THE LEADER of a New Generation of
Personal Development and Leadership Experts

 *Chris Widener is an example of how anyone can overcome any odds to achieve a successful life and help others achieve the same. Chris has overcome many obstacles... living through his father's sudden death when he was four, being sent away from his family to live with relatives at age nine and becoming involved with drugs and alcohol by the age of twelve.*

Chris overcame those obstacles and has been speaking professionally since 1988 and has shared the stage with top political figures, nationally known television news anchors, best-selling authors and professional athletes. He has spoken on motivation and leadership to groups at some of America's finest organizations such as General Electric, Cisco Systems and the Harvard Business School.

Chris has written over 450 articles and 7 books and has produced more than 40 audio programs on leadership and motivation. Chris is the host of the Chris Widener television show and the co-host, along with Zig Ziglar, of the True Performance television show.

Chris, his wife Lisa, and their four children make their home in a suburb of Seattle, Washington.

If you would like more information regarding Chris Widener's corporate booking rates go to www.chriswidener.com or email info@chriswidener.com or call 877-929-0439.

To subscribe to Chris Widener's Free Ezine and to see his complete listing of products go to www.chriswidener.com or email info@chriswidener.com or call 877-929-0439.

Let Chris Widener and Jim Rohn help guide you on your journey through the Twelve Pillars to personal success...

The Jim Rohn One-Year Success Plan:
A Plan of Consistent and Continual Growth!

We have had 99% of our enrollees stay committed to a plan of consistent and continual growth in their personal and professional lives. The statistics and unsolicited testimonials are astonishing! Simply stated, in 39 plus years, we have never witnessed or been able to match the success and opportunity that The Jim Rohn One-Year Success Plan has generated.

The Bronze Package includes:

1. A One-Year Game Plan Covering 12 Pillars of Success (one per month - see below) and Geared to Help You Achieve a 10%-40% Increase in the Following:

Month 1) Personal Development - Become the person you truly desire to be

Month 2) Goal-setting - multiply your long-term success quotient/clearly defined 10-year goals

Month 3) Health - Spiritual/Physical/Emotional - Improve your looks, confidence, energy and quality and length of life

Month 4) Financial Independence/Getting Out of Debt/Saving/Giving

Month 5) Relationships - Become a more effective and loving parent, spouse and friend

Month 6) Time Management - Gain between 10 and 15 additional forty-hour work weeks per year

Month 7) Networking/Referrals - Create more positive influence in the marketplace

Month 8) Selling/Negotiating - Increase your production by 10%-50%

Month 9) Communication/Presentation - Increase every level of performance related to your company, staff and personal relationships

Month 10) Leadership - Multiply your efforts and have a positive influence over a larger sphere of people

Month 11) Accelerated Learning - Quickly improve your skills and aptitude to gain and retain knowledge

Month 12) Legacy/Contribution - Take the time to apply your skills in making a difference in your community and world

2. 52 Unique, Weekly Strategic Game Plans via Email with downloadable workbook pages.

3. Receive 12 Conference Calls (one per month) with a specific focus and hosted by a Premier Expert in each of the 12 Pillars of Success including Jim Rohn, Brian Tracy, Zig Ziglar, Patricia Fripp, Bob Burg, Chris Widener and more...

4. Additional Downloadable Books, Audios, Conference Calls and Weekly Workbook Files.

The Silver Package includes:

All benefits listed in Bronze Package above PLUS:

5. The Jim Rohn Weekend Event - Excelling in the New Millennium on 20 CDs - includes Jim Rohn, Zig Ziglar, Jeffrey Gitomer, Bob Burg (7 speakers total), Jim's complete 2 day program and 8 bonus sessions/3 days total.

The Gold Package includes:

All benefits listed in Silver Package above PLUS:

6. 21 Hours of DVDs from the Jim Rohn Weekend Event - Excelling in the New Millennium - includes Jim Rohn, Zig Ziglar, Jeffrey Gitomer (7 speakers total), Jim's complete 2-day program and 8 bonus sessions/3 days total.

7. Brian Tracy's Success Mastery Academy - 16 Modules on 16 CDs/Comprehensive Workbook

8. The Jim Rohn Leather Journal

9. Special Bonus - mini seminar conference call each quarter with an expert in a specialized field (Finance, Marketing, Leadership, etc.)

For details go to http://oneyear.jimrohn.com
or call 800-929-0434.

*To Order Additional Copies of **Live the Life You Have Always Dreamed Of, The Image** or **Twelve Pillars** by Chris Widener, see quantity discounts below:*

  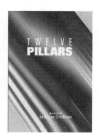

Quantity pricing for paperback:
(Retail $12.95)

1-9	$9.00 ea
10-24	$7.00 ea
25-99	$4.50 ea
100+	$3.00 ea

Quantity pricing for hardback:
(Retail $17.95)

1-9	$12.00 ea
10-24	$9.00 ea
25-99	$6.50 ea
100+	$4.50 ea

Secrets of Influence by Chris Widener
12 Characteristics of Dynamic Leaders, Sales People and Top Performers

This program is based on the Keynote address that Chris Widener gives to organizations all over the world, produced solely to help you learn what the successful already know - how to earn wealth, power, recognition and influence that will change your life forever and allow you to live the life of your dreams!

For a complete listing of Chris Widener's CDs, DVDs, books, MP3s and ebooks, including The Angel Inside, Extraordinary Leaders Seminar (13 CDs), Ultimate Success Series (12 CDs), Twelve Pillars and more, or to order:

Go to ChrisWidener.com and sign up for the Free Ezine!

Or:
1) Call 877-929-0439
2) Email: speaker@ChrisWidener.com
3) Visit us on the Web: www.ChrisWidener.com
4) Via mail: **Chris Widener International**
                  2835 Exchange Blvd., Suite 200
                  Southlake, TX 76092

NEW RELEASE!   *Twelve Pillars Audio Series (7 CDs)*

**Based on Twelve Pillars by Chris Widener
and Jim Rohn**

For more information, go to:
www.ChrisWidener.com/12pillarscds

141

Gifts that Inspire and Tools to Build Your Business...
Excerpts from the Treasury of Quotes

Jim's, Brian's, Zig's or Denis' booklets can be given as a stand-alone gift or enclosed with a gift card or thank you note. They are the perfect addition that will have a positive effect on the recipient and are sure to be kept forever and not thrown away like a note or business card might be. Perfect for customers, family and friends!

Excellent for those of you involved with:

· Real Estate	**· Sales**
· Mortgage	**· Training**
· Insurance	**· Toastmasters**
· Network Marketing	**· Doctors/Dentists**
· Chiropractors	**· Educators/Coaches**

For mix and match pricing, go to YourSuccessStore.com/gifts

The Treasury of Quotes

Features 365 quotes on 60 topics gathered over 40 plus years of wit and wisdom from Jim Rohn. A must for your library!
Burgundy hardback with gold foil lettering.
Retail $20 each
Special $12 each

Go to www.jimrohn.com/products

Building Your Network Marketing Business

The Hottest single CD ever created in the Network Marketing Industry!
Subjects include: Awakening to the Opportunity, Profits are Better than Wages, The Magic of Part-Time, The Set of the Sail, The Law of Averages, The Law of Sowing & Reaping and more! Use for both Training and Recruiting!

To order these products or other products go to
www.jimrohn.com/building or call 800-929-0434.